AF292683

Giles Lytton Strachey

Eminent Victorians

© 2025, Giles Lytton Strachey (domaine public)
Édition : BoD · Books on Demand, 31 avenue Saint-Rémy, 57600 Forbach, bod@bod.fr
Impression : Libri Plureos GmbH, Friedensallee 273, 22763 Hamburg (Allemagne)
ISBN : 978-2-3225-7238-0
Dépôt légal : Avril 2025

Eminent Victorians

By

Giles Lytton Strachey

EMINENT VICTORIANS

Preface

THE history of the Victorian Age will never be written; we know too much about it. For ignorance is the first requisite of the historian—ignorance, which simplifies and clarifies, which selects and omits, with a placid perfection unattainable by the highest art. Concerning the Age which has just passed, our fathers and our grandfathers have poured forth and accumulated so vast a quantity of information that the industry of a Ranke would be submerged by it, and the perspicacity of a Gibbon would quail before it. It is not by the direct method of a scrupulous narration that the explorer of the past can hope to depict that singular epoch. If he is wise, he will adopt a subtler strategy. He will attack his subject in unexpected places; he will fall upon the flank, or the rear; he will shoot a sudden, revealing searchlight into obscure recesses, hitherto undivined. He will row out over that great ocean of material, and lower down into it, here and there, a little bucket, which will bring up to the light of day some characteristic specimen, from those far depths, to be examined with a careful curiosity. Guided by these considerations, I have written the ensuing studies. I have attempted, through the medium of biography, to present some Victorian visions to the modern eye. They are, in one sense, haphazard visions—that is to say, my choice of subjects has been determined by no desire to construct a system or to prove a theory, but by simple motives of convenience and of art. It has been my purpose to illustrate rather than to explain. It would have been futile to hope to tell even a precis of the truth about the Victorian age, for the shortest precis must fill innumerable volumes. But, in the lives of an ecclesiastic, an educational authority, a woman of action, and a man of adventure, I have sought to examine and elucidate certain fragments of the truth which took my fancy and lay to my hand.

I hope, however, that the following pages may prove to be of interest from the strictly biographical, no less than from the historical point of view. Human beings are too important to be treated as mere symptoms of the past. They have a value which is independent of any temporal processes—which is eternal, and must be felt for its own sake. The art of biography seems to have fallen on evil times in England. We have had, it is true, a few masterpieces, but we have never had, like the French, a great biographical tradition; we have had no Fontenelles and Condorcets, with their incomparable eloges, compressing into a few shining pages the manifold existences of men. With us, the most delicate and humane of all the branches of the art of writing has been relegated to the journeymen of letters; we do not reflect that it is perhaps as difficult to write a good life as to live one. Those two fat volumes, with which it is our custom to commemorate the dead—who does not know them, with their ill-digested masses of material, their slipshod style, their tone of tedious panegyric, their lamentable lack of selection, of detachment, of design? They are as familiar as the cortege of the undertaker, and wear the same air of slow, funereal barbarism. One is tempted to suppose, of some of them, that they were composed by that functionary as the final item of his job. The studies in this book are indebted, in more ways than one, to such works—works which certainly deserve the name of Standard Biographies. For they have provided me not only with much indispensable information, but with something even more precious—an example. How many lessons are to be learned from them! But it is hardly necessary to particularise. To preserve, for instance, a becoming brevity—a brevity which excludes everything that is redundant and nothing that is significant—that, surely, is the first duty of the biographer. The second, no less surely, is to maintain his own freedom of spirit. It is not his business to be complimentary; it is his business to lay bare the facts of the case, as he understands them. That is what I have aimed at in this book—to lay bare the facts of some cases, as I understand them, dispassionately, impartially, and without ulterior intentions. To quote the words of a Master—'Je n'impose rien; je ne propose rien: j'expose.'

L.S.

A list of the principal sources from which I have drawn is appended to each Biography. I would indicate, as an honourable exception to the current commodity, Sir Edward Cook's excellent Life of Florence Nightingale, without which my own study, though composed on a very different scale and from a decidedly different angle, could not have been written.

Cardinal Manning

HENRY EDWARD MANNING was born in 1807 and died in 1892. His life was extraordinary in many ways, but its interest for the modern inquirer depends mainly upon two considerations—the light which his career throws upon the spirit of his age, and the psychological problems suggested by his inner history. He belonged to that class of eminent ecclesiastics—and it is by no means a small class—who have been distinguished less for saintliness and learning than for practical ability. Had he lived in the Middle Ages he would certainly have been neither a Francis nor an Aquinas, but he might have been an Innocent. As it was, born in the England of the nineteenth century, growing up in the very seed-time of modern progress, coming to maturity with the first onrush of Liberalism, and living long enough to witness the victories of Science and Democracy, he yet, by a strange concatenation of circumstances, seemed almost to revive in his own person that long line of diplomatic and administrative clerics which, one would have thought, had come to an end for ever with Cardinal Wolsey.

In Manning, so it appeared, the Middle Ages lived again. The tall gaunt figure, with the face of smiling asceticism, the robes, and the biretta, as it passed in triumph from High Mass at the Oratory to philanthropic gatherings at Exeter Hall, from Strike Committees at the Docks to Mayfair drawing-rooms where fashionable ladies knelt to the Prince of the Church, certainly bore witness to a singular condition of affairs. What had happened? Had a dominating character imposed itself upon a hostile environment? Or was the nineteenth century, after all, not so hostile? Was there something in it, scientific and progressive as it was, which went out to welcome the representative of ancient tradition and uncompromising faith? Had it, perhaps, a place in its heart for such as Manning—a soft place, one might almost say? Or, on the other hand, was it he who had been supple and yielding? He who had won by art what he would never have won by force, and who had managed, so to speak, to be one of the leaders of the procession less through merit than through a superior faculty for gliding adroitly to the front rank? And, in any case, by what odd chances, what shifts and struggles, what combinations of circumstance and character, had this old man come to be where he was? Such questions are easier to ask than to answer; but it may be instructive, and even amusing, to look a little more closely into the complexities of so curious a story.

I

UNDOUBTEDLY, what is most obviously striking in the history of Manning's career is the persistent strength of his innate characteristics. Through all the changes of his fortunes the powerful spirit of the man worked on undismayed. It was as if the Fates had laid a wager that they would daunt him; and in the end they lost their bet.

His father was a rich West Indian merchant, a governor of the Bank of England, a Member of Parliament, who drove into town every day from his country seat in a coach and four, and was content with nothing short of a bishop for the christening of his children. Little Henry, like the rest, had his bishop; but he was obliged to wait for him—for as long as eighteen months. In those days, and even a generation later, as Keble bears witness, there was great laxity in regard to the early baptism of children. The delay has been noted by Manning's biographer as the first stumbling-block in the spiritual life of the future Cardinal; but he surmounted it with success.

His father was more careful in other ways.

'His refinement and delicacy of mind were such,' wrote Manning long afterwards, 'that I never heard out of his mouth a word which might not have been spoken in the presence of the most pure and sensitive—except,' he adds, 'on one occasion. He was then forced by others to repeat a negro story which, though free from all evil de sexu, was indelicate. He did it with great resistance. His example gave me a hatred of all such talk.'

The family lived in an atmosphere of Evangelical piety. One day the little boy came in from the farmyard, and his mother asked him whether he had seen the peacock. 'I said yes, and the nurse said no, and my mother made me kneel down and beg God to forgive me for not speaking the truth.' At the age of four the child was told by a cousin of the age of six that 'God had a book in which He wrote down everything we did wrong. This so terrified me for days that I remember being found by my mother sitting under a kind of writing-table in great fear. I never forgot this at any time in my life,' the Cardinal tells us, 'and it has been a great grace to me.' When he was nine years old he 'devoured the Apocalypse; and I never all through my life forgot the "lake that burneth with fire and brimstone". That verse has kept me like an audible voice through all my life, and through worlds of danger in my youth.'

At Harrow the worlds of danger were already around him; but yet he listened to the audible voice. 'At school and college I never failed to say my prayers, so far as memory serves me, even for a day.' And he underwent another religious experience: he read Paley's Evidences. 'I took in the whole argument,' wrote Manning, when he was over seventy, 'and I thank God that nothing has ever shaken it.' Yet on the whole he led the unspiritual life of an ordinary schoolboy. We have glimpses of him as a handsome lad, playing cricket, or strutting about in tasselled Hessian top-boots. And on one occasion at least he gave proof of a certain dexterity of conduct which deserved to be remembered. He went out of bounds, and a master, riding by and seeing him on the other side of a field, tied his horse to a gate, and ran after him. The astute youth outran the master, fetched a circle, reached the gate, jumped on to the horse's back and rode off. For this he was very properly chastised; but, of what use was chastisement? No whipping, however severe, could have eradicated from little Henry's mind a quality at least as firmly planted in it as his fear of Hell and his belief in the arguments of Paley.

It had been his father's wish that Manning should go into the Church; but the thought disgusted him; and when he reached Oxford, his tastes, his ambitions, his successes at the Union, all seemed to mark him out for a political career. He was a year junior to Samuel Wilberforce, and a year senior to Gladstone. In those days the Union was the recruiting-ground for young politicians; Ministers came down from London to listen to the debates; and a few years later the Duke of Newcastle gave Gladstone a pocket borough on the strength of his speech at the Union against the Reform Bill. To those three young men, indeed, the whole world lay open. Were they not rich, well-connected, and endowed with an infinite capacity for making speeches? The event justified the highest expectations of their friends; for the least distinguished of the three died a bishop. The only danger lay in another direction.

'Watch, my dear Samuel,' wrote the elder Wilberforce to his son, 'watch with jealousy whether you find yourself unduly solicitous about acquitting yourself; whether you are too much chagrined when you fail, or are puffed up by your success. Undue solicitude about popular estimation is a weakness against which all real Christians must guard with the utmost jealous watchfulness. The more you can retain the impression of your being surrounded by a cloud of witnesses of the invisible world, to use the scripture phrase, the more you will be armed against this besetting sin.'

But suddenly it seemed as if such a warning could, after all, have very little relevance to Manning; for, on his leaving Oxford, the brimming cup was dashed from his lips. He was already beginning to dream of himself in the House of Commons, the solitary advocate of some great cause whose triumph was to be eventually brought about by his extraordinary efforts, when his father was declared a bankrupt, and all his hopes of a political career came to an end forever.

It was at this time that Manning became intimate with a pious lady, the sister of one of his College friends, whom he used to describe as his Spiritual Mother. He made her his confidante; and one day, as they walked together in the shrubbery, he revealed the bitterness of the disappointment into which his father's failure had plunged him. She tried to cheer him, and then she added that there were higher aims open to him which he had not considered. 'What do you mean?' he asked. 'The kingdom of Heaven,' she answered; 'heavenly ambitions are not closed against you.' The young man listened, was silent, and said at last that he did not know but she was right. She suggested reading the Bible together; and they accordingly did so during the whole of that Vacation, every morning after breakfast. Yet, in spite of these devotional exercises, and in spite of a voluminous correspondence on religious subjects with his Spiritual Mother, Manning still continued to indulge in secular hopes. He entered the Colonial Office as a supernumerary clerk, and it was only when the offer of a Merton Fellowship seemed to depend upon his taking orders that his heavenly ambitions began to assume a definite shape. Just then he fell in love with Miss Deffell, whose father would have nothing to say to a young man without prospects, and forbade him the house. It was only too true; what WERE the prospects of a supernumerary clerk in the Colonial Office? Manning went to Oxford and took orders. He was elected to the Merton Fellowship, and obtained through the influence of the Wilberforces a curacy in Sussex. At the last moment he almost drew back. 'I think the whole step has been too precipitate,' he wrote to his brother-in-law. 'I have rather allowed the instance of my friends, and the allurements of an agreeable curacy in many respects, to get the better of my sober judgment.' His vast ambitions, his dreams of public service, of honours, and of power, was all this to end in a little country curacy 'agreeable in many respects'? But there was nothing for it; the deed was done; and the Fates had apparently succeeded very effectively in getting rid of Manning. All he could do was to make the best of a bad business.

Accordingly, in the first place, he decided that he had received a call from God 'ad veritatem et ad seipsum'; and, in the second, forgetting Miss Deffell, he married his rector's daughter. Within a few months the rector died, and Manning stepped into his shoes; and at least it could be said that the shoes were not uncomfortable. For the next seven years he fulfilled the functions of a country clergyman. He was energetic and devout; he was polite and handsome; his fame grew in the diocese. At last he began to be spoken of as the probable successor to the old Archdeacon of Chichester. When Mrs. Manning prematurely died, he was at first inconsolable, but he found relief in the distraction of redoubled work. How could he have guessed that one day he would come to number that loss among 'God's special mercies? Yet so it was to be. In after years, the memory of his wife seemed to be blotted from his mind; he never spoke of her; every letter, every record, of his married life he

destroyed; and when word was sent to him that her grave was falling into ruin:
'It is best so,' the Cardinal answered, 'let it be. Time effaces all things.' But,
when the grave was yet fresh, the young Rector would sit beside it, day after
day, writing his sermons.

II

IN the meantime, a series of events was taking place in another part of
England, which was to have a no less profound effect upon Manning's history
than the merciful removal of his wife. In the same year in which he took up his
Sussex curacy, the Tracts for the Times had begun to appear at Oxford. The
'Oxford Movement', in fact, had started on its course. The phrase is still
familiar; but its meaning has become somewhat obscured both by the lapse of
time and the intrinsic ambiguity of the subjects connected with it. Let us
borrow for a moment the wings of Historic Imagination, and, hovering lightly
over the Oxford of the thirties, take a rapid bird's-eye view.

For many generations the Church of England had slept the sleep of the …
comfortable. The sullen murmurings of dissent, the loud battle-cry of
Revolution, had hardly disturbed her slumbers. Portly divines subscribed with
a sigh or a smile to the Thirty-nine Articles, sank quietly into easy living, rode
gaily to hounds of a morning as gentlemen should, and, as gentlemen should,
carried their two bottles of an evening. To be in the Church was in fact simply
to pursue one of those professions which Nature and Society had decided were
proper to gentlemen and gentlemen alone. The fervours of piety, the zeal of
Apostolic charity, the enthusiasm of self-renunciation—these things were all
very well in their way and in their place; but their place was certainly not the
Church of England. Gentlemen were neither fervid nor zealous, and above all
they were not enthusiastic. There were, it was true, occasionally to be found
within the Church some strait-laced parsons of the high Tory school who
looked back with regret to the days of Laud or talked of the Apostolical
Succession; and there were groups of square-toed Evangelicals who were
earnest over the Atonement, confessed to a personal love of Jesus Christ, and
seemed to have arranged the whole of their lives, down to the minutest details
of act and speech, with reference to Eternity. But such extremes were the rare
exceptions. The great bulk of the clergy walked calmly along the smooth road
of ordinary duty. They kept an eye on the poor of the parish, and they
conducted the Sunday Services in a becoming manner; for the rest, they
differed neither outwardly nor inwardly from the great bulk of the laity, to
whom the Church was a useful organisation for the maintenance of Religion,
as by law established.

The awakening came at last, however, and it was a rude one. The liberal principles of the French Revolution, checked at first in the terrors of reaction, began to make their way into England. Rationalists lifted up their heads; Bentham and the Mills propounded Utilitarianism; the Reform Bill was passed; and there were rumours abroad of disestablishment. Even Churchmen seemed to have caught the infection. Dr. Whately was so bold as to assert that, in the interpretation of Scripture, different opinions might be permitted upon matters of doubt; and, Dr. Arnold drew up a disquieting scheme for allowing Dissenters into the Church, though it is true that he did not go quite so far as to contemplate the admission of Unitarians.

At this time, there was living in a country parish, a young clergyman of the name of John Keble. He had gone to Oxford at the age of fifteen, where, after a successful academic career, he had been made a Fellow of Oriel. He had then returned to his father's parish and taken up the duties of a curate. He had a thorough knowledge of the contents of the Prayer-book, the ways of a Common Room, the conjugations of the Greek Irregular Verbs, and the small jests of a country parsonage; and the defects of his experience in other directions were replaced by a zeal and a piety which were soon to prove themselves equal, and more than equal, to whatever calls might be made upon them. The superabundance of his piety overflowed into verse; and the holy simplicity of the Christian Year carried his name into the remotest lodging-houses of England.

As for his zeal, however, it needed another outlet. Looking forth upon the doings of his fellow-men through his rectory windows in Gloucestershire, Keble felt his whole soul shaken with loathing, anger, and dread. Infidelity was stalking through the land; authority was laughed at; the hideous doctrines of Democracy were being openly preached. Worse still, if possible, the Church herself was ignorant and lukewarm; she had forgotten the mysteries of the sacraments, she had lost faith in the Apostolical Succession; she was no longer interested in the Early Fathers; and she submitted herself to the control of a secular legislature, the members of which were not even bound to profess belief in the Atonement. In the face of such enormities what could Keble do? He was ready to do anything, but he was a simple and an unambitious man, and his wrath would in all probability have consumed itself unappeased within him had he not chanced to come into contact, at the critical moment, with a spirit more excitable and daring than his own.

Hurrell Froude, one of Keble's pupils, was a clever young man to whom had fallen a rather larger share of self-assurance and intolerance than even clever young men usually possess. What was singular about him, however, was not so much his temper as his tastes. The sort of ardour which impels more normal youths to haunt Music Halls and fall in love with actresses took the form, in

Froude's case, of a romantic devotion to the Deity and an intense interest in the state of his own soul. He was obsessed by the ideals of saintliness, and convinced of the supreme importance of not eating too much. He kept a diary in which he recorded his delinquencies, and they were many. 'I cannot say much for myself today,' he writes on September 29th, 1826 (he was twenty-three years old). 'I did not read the Psalms and Second Lesson after breakfast, which I had neglected to do before, though I had plenty of time on my hands. Would have liked to be thought adventurous for a scramble I had at the Devil's Bridge. Looked with greediness to see if there was a goose on the table for dinner; and though what I ate was of the plainest sort, and I took no variety, yet even this was partly the effect of accident, and I certainly rather exceeded in quantity, as I was fuzzy and sleepy after dinner.' 'I allowed myself to be disgusted, with—'s pomposity,' he writes a little later, 'also smiled at an allusion in the Lessons to abstemiousness in eating. I hope not from pride or vanity, but mistrust; it certainly was unintentional.' And again, 'As to my meals, I can say that I was always careful to see that no one else would take a thing before I served myself; and I believe as to the kind of my food, a bit of cold endings of a dab at breakfast, and a scrap of mackerel at dinner, are the only things that diverged from the strict rule of simplicity.' 'I am obliged to confess,' he notes, 'that in my intercourse with the Supreme Being, I am be come more and more sluggish.' And then he exclaims: 'Thine eye trieth my inward parts, and knoweth my thoughts … Oh that my ways were made so direct that I might keep Thy statutes. I will walk in Thy Commandments when Thou hast set my heart at liberty.'

Such were the preoccupations of this young man. Perhaps they would have been different, if he had had a little less of what Newman describes as his 'high severe idea of the intrinsic excellence of Virginity'; but it is useless to speculate.

Naturally enough the fierce and burning zeal of Keble had a profound effect upon his mind. The two became intimate friends, and Froude, eagerly seizing upon the doctrines of the elder man, saw to it that they had as full a measure of controversial notoriety as an Oxford common room could afford. He plunged the metaphysical mysteries of the Holy Catholic Church into the atmosphere of party politics. Surprised Doctors of Divinity found themselves suddenly faced with strange questions which had never entered their heads before. Was the Church of England, or was it not, a part of the Church Catholic? If it was, were not the Reformers of the sixteenth century renegades? Was not the participation of the Body and Blood of Christ essential to the maintenance of Christian life and hope in each individual? Were Timothy and Titus Bishops? Or were they not? If they were, did it not follow that the power of administering the Holy Eucharist was the attribute of a sacred order founded by Christ Himself? Did not the Fathers refer to the tradition of the Church as to something independent of the written word, and sufficient to refute heresy, even alone? Was it not, therefore, God's unwritten word? And did it not demand the same reverence from us as the Scriptures, and for exactly the same reason—BECAUSE IT WAS HIS WORD? The Doctors of Divinity were aghast at such questions, which seemed to lead they hardly knew whither; and they found it difficult to think of very apposite answers. But Hurrell Froude supplied the answers himself readily enough. All Oxford, all England, should know the truth. The time was out of joint, and he was only too delighted to have been born to set it right.

But, after all, something more was needed than even the excitement of Froude combined with the conviction of Keble to ruffle seriously the vast calm waters of Christian thought; and it so happened that that thing was not wanting: it was the genius of John Henry Newman. If Newman had never lived, or if his father, when the gig came round on the fatal morning, still undecided between the two Universities, had chanced to turn the horse's head in the direction of Cambridge, who can doubt that the Oxford Movement would have flickered out its little flame unobserved in the Common Room of Oriel? And how different, too, would have been the fate of Newman himself! He was a child of the Romantic Revival, a creature of emotion and of memory, a dreamer whose secret spirit dwelt apart in delectable mountains, an artist whose subtle senses caught, like a shower in the sunshine, the impalpable rainbow of the immaterial world. In other times, under other skies, his days would have been more fortunate. He might have helped to weave the garland of Meleager, or to mix the lapis lazuli of Fra Angelico, or to chase the delicate truth in the shade of an Athenian palaestra, or his hands might have fashioned those ethereal faces that smile in the niches of Chartres. Even in his own age he might, at Cambridge, whose cloisters have ever been consecrated to poetry and common sense, have followed quietly in Gray's footsteps and brought into flower those seeds of inspiration which now lie embedded amid the faded devotion of the Lyra Apostolica.

At Oxford, he was doomed. He could not withstand the last enchantment of the Middle Age. It was in vain that he plunged into the pages of Gibbon or communed for long hours with Beethoven over his beloved violin. The air was thick with clerical sanctity, heavy with the odours of tradition and the soft warmth of spiritual authority; his friendship with Hurrell Froude did the rest. All that was weakest in him hurried him onward, and all that was strongest in him too. His curious and vaulting imagination began to construct vast philosophical fabrics out of the writings of ancient monks, and to dally with visions of angelic visitations and the efficacy of the oil of St Walburga; his emotional nature became absorbed in the partisan passions of a University clique; and his subtle intellect concerned itself more and more exclusively with the dialectical splitting of dogmatical hairs. His future course was marked out for him all too clearly; and yet by a singular chance the true nature of the man was to emerge triumphant in the end. If Newman had died at the age of sixty, today he would have been already forgotten, save by a few ecclesiastical historians; but he lived to write his Apologia, and to reach immortality, neither as a thinker nor as a theologian, but as an artist who has embalmed the poignant history of an intensely human spirit in the magical spices of words.

When Froude succeeded in impregnating Newman with the ideas of Keble, the Oxford Movement began. The original and remarkable characteristic of these three men was that they took the Christian Religion au pied de la lettre. This had not been done in England for centuries. When they declared every Sunday that they believed in the Holy Catholic Church, they meant it. When they repeated the Athanasian Creed, they meant it. Even, when they subscribed to the Thirty-nine Articles, they meant it-or at least they thought they did. Now such a state of mind was dangerous—more dangerous indeed—than they at first realised. They had started with the innocent assumption that the Christian Religion was contained in the doctrines of the Church of England; but, the more they examined this matter, the more difficult and dubious it became. The Church of England bore everywhere upon it the signs of human imperfection; it was the outcome of revolution and of compromise, of the exigencies of politicians and the caprices of princes, of the prejudices of theologians and the necessities of the State. How had it happened that this piece of patchwork had become the receptacle for the august and infinite mysteries of the Christian Faith? This was the problem with which Newman and his friends found themselves confronted. Other men might, and apparently did, see nothing very strange in such a situation; but other men saw in Christianity itself scarcely more than a convenient and respectable appendage to existence, by which a sound system of morals was inculcated, and through which one might hope to attain to everlasting bliss.

To Newman and Keble it was otherwise. They saw a transcendent manifestation of Divine power flowing down elaborate and immense through the ages; a consecrated priesthood, stretching back, through the mystic symbol of the laying on of hands, to the very Godhead; a whole universe of spiritual beings brought into communion with the Eternal by means of wafers; a great mass of metaphysical doctrines, at once incomprehensible and of incalculable import, laid down with infinite certitude; they saw the supernatural everywhere and at all times, a living force, floating invisible in angels, inspiring saints, and investing with miraculous properties the commonest material things. No wonder that they found such a spectacle hard to bring into line with the institution which had been evolved from the divorce of Henry VIII, the intrigues of Elizabethan parliaments, and the Revolution of 1688. They did, no doubt, soon satisfy themselves that they had succeeded in this apparently hopeless task; but, the conclusions which they came to in order to do so were decidedly startling.

The Church of England, they declared, was indeed the one true Church, but she had been under an eclipse since the Reformation; in fact, since she had begun to exist. She had, it is true, escaped the corruptions of Rome; but she had become enslaved by the secular power, and degraded by the false doctrines of Protestantism. The Christian Religion was still preserved intact by the English priesthood, but it was preserved, as it were, unconsciously—a priceless deposit, handed down blindly from generation to generation, and subsisting less by the will of man than through the ordinance of God as expressed in the mysterious virtue of the Sacraments. Christianity, in short, had become entangled in a series of unfortunate circumstances from which it was the plain duty of Newman and his friends to rescue it forthwith. What was curious was that this task had been reserved, in so marked a manner, for them. Some of the divines of the seventeenth century had, perhaps, been vouchsafed glimpses of the truth; but they were glimpses and nothing more. No, the waters of the true Faith had dived underground at the Reformation, and they were waiting for the wand of Newman to strike the rock before they should burst forth once more into the light of day. The whole matter, no doubt, was Providential—what other explanation could there be?

The first step, it was clear, was to purge the Church of her shames and her errors. The Reformers must be exposed; the yoke of the secular power must be thrown off; dogma must be reinstated in its old pre-eminence; and Christians must be reminded of what they had apparently forgotten—the presence of the supernatural in daily life. 'It would be a gain to this country,' Keble observed, 'were it vastly more superstitious, more bigoted, more gloomy, more fierce in its religion, than at present it shows itself to be.' 'The only good I know of Cranmer,' said Hurrell Froude, 'was that he burned well.' Newman preached, and soon the new views began to spread. Among the earliest of the converts was Dr Pusey, a man of wealth and learning, a professor, a canon of Christ Church, who had, it was rumoured, been to Germany. Then the Tracts for the Times were started under Newman's editorship, and the Movement was launched upon the world.

The Tracts were written 'with the hope of rousing members of our Church to comprehend her alarming position ... as a man might give notice of a fire or inundation, to startle all who heard him'. They may be said to have succeeded in their objective, for the sensation which they caused among clergymen throughout the country was extreme. They dealt with a great variety of questions, but the underlying intention of all of them was to attack the accepted doctrines and practices of the Church of England. Dr. Pusey wrote learnedly on Baptismal Regeneration; he also wrote on Fasting. His treatment of the latter subject met with considerable disapproval, which surprised the

Doctor. 'I was not prepared,' he said, 'for people questioning, even in the abstract, the duty of fasting; I thought serious-minded persons at least supposed they practised fasting in some way or other. I assumed the duty to be acknowledged and thought it only undervalued.' We live and learn, even though we have been to Germany.

Other tracts discussed the Holy Catholic Church, the Clergy, and the Liturgy. One treated of the question 'whether a clergyman of the Church of England be now bound to have morning and evening prayers daily in his parish church?' Another pointed out the 'Indications of a superintending Providence in the preservation of the Prayer-book and in the changes which it has undergone'. Another consisted of a collection of 'Advent Sermons on Antichrist'. Keble wrote a long and elaborate tract 'On the Mysticism attributed to the Early Fathers of the Church', in which he expressed his opinions upon a large number of curious matters.

'According to men's usual way of talking,' he wrote, 'it would be called an accidental circumstance that there were five loaves, not more nor less, in the store of Our Lord and His disciples wherewith to provide the miraculous feast. But the ancient interpreters treat it as designed and providential, in this surely not erring: and their conjecture is that it represents the sacrifice of the whole world of sense, and especially of the Old Dispensation, which, being outward and visible, might be called the dispensation of the senses, to the FATHER of our LORD JESUS CHRIST, to be a pledge and means of communion with Him according to the terms of the new or evangelical law.

They arrived at this idea by considering the number five, the number of the senses, as the mystical opponent of the visible and sensible universe—ta aistheta, as distinguished from ta noita. Origen lays down the rule in express terms. '"The number five,"' he says, '"frequently, nay almost always, is taken for the five senses."' In another passage, Keble deals with an even more recondite question. He quotes the teaching of St. Barnabas that 'Abraham, who first gave men circumcision, did thereby perform a spiritual and typical action, looking forward to the Son'. St. Barnabas's argument is as follows: Abraham circumcised of his house men to the number of 318. Why 318? Observe first the 18, then the 300. Of the two letters which stand for 18, 10 is represented by 1, 8 by H. 'Thou hast here,' says St. Barnabas, 'the word of Jesus.' As for the 300, 'the Cross is represented by Tau, and the letter Tau represents that number'.

Unfortunately, however, St. Barnabas's premise was of doubtful validity, as the Rev. Mr. Maitland pointed out, in a pamphlet impugning the conclusions of the Tract. 'The simple fact is,' he wrote, 'that when Abraham pursued Chedorlaomer "he armed his trained servants, BORN IN HIS OWN HOUSE, three hundred and eighteen". When, more than thirteen (according to the common chronology, fifteen) years after, he circumcised "all the men of his house, BORN IN THE HOUSE, AND BOUGHT WITH MONEY OF THE STRANGER", and, in fact, every male who was as much as eight days old, we are not told what the number amounted to. Shall we suppose (just for the sake of the interpretation) that Abraham's family had so dwindled in the interval as that now all the males of his household, trained men, slaves, and children, equalled only and exactly the number of his warriors fifteen years before?'

The question seems difficult to answer, but Keble had, as a matter of fact, forestalled the argument in the following passage, which had apparently escaped the notice of the Rev. Mr. Maitland:

'Now whether the facts were really so or not (if it were, it was surely by special providence), that Abraham's household at the time of the circumcision was exactly the same number as before; still the argument of St. Barnabas will stand. As thus: circumcision had from the beginning, a reference to our SAVIOUR, as in other respects, so in this; that the mystical number, which is the cipher of Jesus crucified, was the number of the first circumcised household in the strength of which Abraham prevailed against the powers of the world. So St. Clement of Alexandria, as cited by Fell.'

And Keble supports his contention through ten pages of close print, with references to Aristeas, St. Augustine, St. Jerome, and Dr. Whitby.

Writings of this kind could not fail in their effect. Pious youths in Oxford were carried away by them, and began to flock around the standard of Newman. Newman himself became a party chief—encouraging, organising, persuading. His long black figure, swiftly passing through the streets, was pointed at with awe; crowds flocked to his sermons; his words were repeated from mouth to mouth; 'Credo in Newmannum' became a common catchword. Jokes were made about the Church of England, and practices, unknown for centuries, began to be revived. Young men fasted and did penance, recited the hours of the Roman Breviary, and confessed their sins to Dr. Pusey. Nor was the movement confined to Oxford; it spread in widening circles through the parishes of England; the dormant devotion of the country was suddenly aroused. The new strange notion of taking Christianity literally was delightful to earnest minds; but it was also alarming. Really to mean every word you said, when you repeated the Athanasian Creed! How wonderful! And what enticing and mysterious vistas burst upon the view! But then, those vistas, where were they leading? Supposing—oh heavens!—supposing after all they were to lead to—!

III

IN due course, the Tracts made their appearance at the remote rectory in Sussex. Manning was some years younger than Newman, and the two men had only met occasionally at the University; but now, through common friends, a closer relationship began to grow up between them. It was only to be expected that Newman should be anxious to enroll the rising young Rector among his followers; and, on Manning's side, there were many causes which impelled him to accept the overtures from Oxford.

He was a man of a serious and vigorous temperament, to whom it was inevitable that the bold high principles of the Movement should strongly appeal. There was also an element in his mind that element which had terrified him in his childhood with Apocalyptic visions, and urged him in his youth to Bible readings after breakfast—which now brought him under the spell of the Oxford theories of sacramental mysticism. And besides, the Movement offered another attraction: it imputed an extraordinary, transcendent merit to the profession which Manning himself pursued. The cleric was not as his lay brethren; he was a creature apart, chosen by Divine will and sanctified by Divine mysteries. It was a relief to find, when one had supposed that one was nothing but a clergyman, that one might, after all, be something else—one might be a priest.

Accordingly, Manning shook off his early Evangelical convictions, started an active correspondence with Newman, and was soon working for the new cause. He collected quotations, and began to translate the works of Optatus for Dr. Pusey. He wrote an article on Justin for the British Critic, "Newman's Magazine". He published a sermon on Faith, with notes and appendices, which was condemned by an evangelical bishop, and fiercely attacked by no less a person than the celebrated Mr. Bowdler. 'The sermon,' said Mr Bowdler, in a book which he devoted to the subject, 'was bad enough, but the appendix was abominable.' At the same time he was busy asserting the independence of the Church of England, opposing secular education, and bringing out pamphlets against the Ecclesiastical Commission, which had been appointed by Parliament to report on Church Property. Then we find him in the role of a spiritual director of souls. Ladies met him by stealth in his church, and made their confessions. Over one case—that of a lady, who found herself drifting towards Rome—he consulted Newman. Newman advised him to 'enlarge upon the doctrine of I Cor. vii';

'also, I think you must press on her the prospect of benefiting the poor Church, through which she has her baptism, by stopping in it. Does she not care for the souls of all around her, steeped and stifled in Protestantism? How will she best care for them by indulging her own feelings in the communion of Rome, or in denying herself, and staying in sackcloth and ashes to do them good?'

Whether these arguments were successful does not appear.

For several years after his wife's death, Manning was occupied with these new activities, while his relations with Newman developed into what was apparently a warm friendship. 'And now vive valeque, my dear Manning', we find Newman writing in a letter dated 'in festo S. Car. 1838', 'as wishes and prays yours affectionately, John H. Newman'. But, as time went on, the situation became more complicated. Tractarianism began to arouse the hostility, not only of the evangelical, but of the moderate churchmen, who could not help perceiving in the ever-deepening, 'catholicism' of the Oxford party, the dread approaches of Rome. The "Record" newspaper an influential Evangelical journal—took up the matter and sniffed Popery in every direction; it spoke of certain clergymen as 'tainted'; and after that, preferment seemed to pass those clergymen by. The fact that Manning found it wise to conduct his confessional ministrations in secret was in itself highly significant. It was necessary to be careful, and Manning was very careful indeed. The neighbouring Archdeacon, Mr. Hare, was a low churchman; Manning made friends with him, as warmly, it seemed, as he had made friends with Newman. He corresponded with him, asked his advice about the books he should read, and discussed questions of Theology—'As to Gal. vi 15, we cannot differ…. With a man who reads and reasons I can have no controversy; and you do both.' Archdeacon Hare was pleased, but soon a rumour reached him, which was, to say the least of it, upsetting. Manning had been removing the high pews from a church in Brighton, and putting in open benches in their place. Everyone knew what that meant; everyone knew that a high pew was one of the bulwarks of Protestantism, and that an open bench had upon it the taint of Rome. But Manning hastened to explain:

'My dear friend,' he wrote, 'I did not exchange pews for open benches, but got the pews (the same in number) moved from the nave of the church to the walls of the side aisles, so that the whole church has a regular arrangement of open benches, which (irregularly) existed before … I am not today quite well, so farewell, with much regard—Yours ever, H. E. M.'

Archdeacon Hare was reassured.

It was important that he should be, for the Archdeacon of Chichester was growing very old, and Hare's influence might be exceedingly useful when a vacancy occurred. So, indeed, it fell out. A new bishop, Dr. Shuttleworth, was appointed to the See, and the old Archdeacon took the opportunity of retiring. Manning was obviously marked out as his successor, but the new bishop happened to be a low churchman, an aggressive low churchman, who went so far as to parody the Tractarian fashion of using Saints' days for the dating of letters by writing 'The Palace, washing-day', at the beginning of his. And— what was equally serious—his views were shared by Mrs. Shuttleworth, who had already decided that the pushing young Rector was 'tainted'. But at the critical moment Archdeacon Hare came to the rescue; he persuaded the Bishop that Manning was safe; and the appointment was accordingly made—behind Mrs. Shuttleworth's back. She was furious, but it was too late; Manning was an Archdeacon. All the lady could do, to indicate her disapprobation, was to put a copy of Mr. Bowdler's book in a conspicuous position on the drawing-room table, when he came to pay his respects at the Palace.

Among the letters of congratulation which Manning received, was one from Mr Gladstone, with whom he had remained on terms of close friendship since their days together at Oxford.

'I rejoice,' Mr Gladstone wrote, 'on your account personally; but more for the sake of the Church. All my brothers-in-law are here and scarcely less delighted than I am. With great glee am I about to write your new address; but, the occasion really calls for higher sentiments; and sure am I that you are one of the men to whom it is specially given to develop the solution of that great problem—how all our minor distractions are to be either abandoned, absorbed, or harmonised through the might of the great principle of communion in the body of Christ.'

Manning was an Archdeacon; but he was not yet out of the woods. His relations with the Tractarians had leaked out, and the Record was beginning to be suspicious. If Mrs. Shuttleworth's opinion of him were to become general, it would certainly be a grave matter. Nobody could wish to live and die a mere Archdeacon. And then, at that very moment, an event occurred which made it imperative to take a definite step, one way or the other. That event was the publication of Tract No. 90.

For some time it had been obvious to every impartial onlooker that Newman was slipping down an inclined plane at the bottom of which lay one thing, and one thing only—the Roman Catholic Church. What was surprising was the length of time which he was taking to reach the inevitable destination. Years passed before he came to realise that his grandiose edifice of a Church Universal would crumble to pieces if one of its foundation stones was to be an amatory intrigue of Henry VIII. But, at last he began to see that terrible monarch glowering at him wherever he turned his eyes. First he tried to exorcise the spectre with the rolling periods of the Caroline divines; but it only strutted the more truculently. Then in despair he plunged into the writings of the early Fathers, and sought to discover some way out of his difficulties in the complicated labyrinth of ecclesiastical history. After months spent in the study of the Monophysite heresy, the alarming conclusion began to force itself upon him that the Church of England was perhaps in schism. Eventually he read an article by a Roman Catholic on St. Augustine and the Donatists, which seemed to put the matter beyond doubt. St. Augustine, in the fifth century, had pointed out that the Donatists were heretics because the Bishop of Rome had said so.

The argument was crushing; it rang in Newman's ears for days and nights; and, though he continued to linger on in agony for six years more, he never could discover any reply to it. All he could hope to do was to persuade himself and anyone else who liked to listen to him that the holding of Anglican orders was not inconsistent with a belief in the whole cycle of Roman doctrine as laid down at the Council of Trent. In this way he supposed that he could at once avoid the deadly sin of heresy and conscientiously remain a clergyman in the Church of England; and with this end in view, he composed Tract No. 90.

The object of the Tract was to prove that there was nothing in the Thirty-nine Articles incompatible with the creed of the Roman Church. Newman pointed out, for instance, that it was generally supposed that the Articles condemned the doctrine of Purgatory; but they did not; they merely condemned the Romish doctrine of Purgatory—and Romish, clearly, was not the same thing as Roman. Hence it followed that believers in the Roman doctrine of Purgatory might subscribe the Articles with a good conscience. Similarly, the Articles condemned 'the sacrifices of masses', but they did not condemn 'the sacrifice of the Mass'. Thus, the Mass might be lawfully celebrated in English Churches. Newman took the trouble to examine the Articles in detail from this point of view, and the conclusion he came to in every case supported his contention in a singular manner.

The Tract produced an immense sensation, for it seemed to be a deadly and treacherous blow aimed at the very heart of the Church of England. Deadly it certainly was, but it was not so treacherous as it appeared at first sight. The members of the English Church had ingenuously imagined up to that moment that it was possible to contain, in a frame of words, the subtle essence of their complicated doctrinal system, involving the mysteries of the Eternal and the Infinite on the one hand, and the elaborate adjustments of temporal government on the other. They did not understand that verbal definitions in such a case will only perform their functions so long as there is no dispute about the matters which they are intended to define: that is to say, so long as there is no need for them. For generations this had been the case with the Thirty-nine Articles. Their drift was clear enough; and nobody bothered over their exact meaning. But directly someone found it important to give them a new and untraditional interpretation, it appeared that they were a mass of ambiguity, and might be twisted into meaning very nearly anything that anybody liked. Steady-going churchmen were appalled and outraged when they saw Newman, in Tract No. 90, performing this operation. But, after all, he was only taking the Church of England at its word. And indeed, since Newman showed the way, the operation has become so exceedingly common that the most steady-going churchman hardly raises an eyebrow at it now.

At the time, however, Newman's treatment of the Articles seemed to display not only a perverted supersubtlety of intellect, but a temper of mind that was fundamentally dishonest. It was then that he first began to be assailed by those charges of untruthfulness which reached their culmination more than twenty years later in the celebrated controversy with Charles Kingsley, which led to the writing of the Apologia. The controversy was not a very fruitful one, chiefly because Kingsley could no more understand the nature of Newman's intelligence than a subaltern in a line regiment can understand a Brahmin of Benares. Kingsley was a stout Protestant, whose hatred of Popery was, at bottom, simply ethical—an honest, instinctive horror of the practices of priestcraft and the habits of superstition; and it was only natural that he should see in those innumerable delicate distinctions which Newman was perpetually drawing, and which he himself had not only never thought of, but could not even grasp, simply another manifestation of the inherent falsehood of Rome. But, in reality, no one, in one sense of the word, was more truthful than Newman. The idea of deceit would have been abhorrent to him; and indeed it was owing to his very desire to explain what he had in his mind exactly and completely, with all the refinements of which his subtle brain was capable, that persons such as Kingsley were puzzled into thinking him dishonest. Unfortunately, however, the possibilities of truth and falsehood depend upon other things besides sincerity. A man may be of a scrupulous and impeccable honesty, and yet his respect for the truth—it cannot be denied—may be insufficient. He may be, like the lunatic, the lover, and the poet, 'of imagination all compact'; he may be blessed, or cursed, with one of those 'seething brains', one of those 'shaping fanatasies' that 'apprehend more than cool reason ever comprehends'; he may be by nature incapable of sifting evidence, or by predilection simply indisposed to do so. 'When we were there,' wrote Newman in a letter to a friend after his conversion, describing a visit to Naples, and the miraculous circumstances connected with the liquefaction of St. Januarius's blood,

'the feast of St. Gennaro was coming on, and the Jesuits were eager for us to stop—they have the utmost confidence in the miracle—and were the more eager because many Catholics, till they have seen it, doubt it. Our father director here tells us that before he went to Naples he did not believe it. That is, they have vague ideas of natural means, exaggeration, etc., not of course imputing fraud. They say conversions often take place in consequence. It is exposed for the Octave, and the miracle continues—it is not simple liquefaction, but sometimes it swells, sometimes boils, sometimes melts—no one can tell what is going to take place. They say it is quite overcoming-and people cannot help crying to see it. I understand that Sir H. Davy attended everyday, and it was this extreme variety of the phenomenon which convinced him that nothing physical would account for it. Yet there is this remarkable fact that liquefactions of blood are common at Naples—and, unless it is irreverent to the Great Author of Miracles to be obstinate in the inquiry, the question certainly rises whether there is something in the air. (Mind, I don't believe there is—and, speaking humbly, and without having seen it, think it a true miracle—but I am arguing.) We saw the blood of St Patrizia, half liquid; i.e. liquefying, on her feast day. St John Baptist's blood sometimes liquefies on the 29th of August, and did when we were at Naples, but we had not time to go to the church. We saw the liquid blood of an Oratorian Father; a good man, but not a saint, who died two centuries ago, I think; and we saw the liquid blood of Da Ponte, the great and holy Jesuit, who, I suppose, was almost a saint. But these instances do not account for liquefaction on certain days, if this is the case. But the most strange phenomenon is what happens at Ravello, a village or town above Amalfi. There is the blood of St. Pantaleon. It is in a vessel amid the stonework of the Altar-it is not touched but on his feast in June it liquefies. And more, there is an excommunication against those who bring portions of the True Cross into the Church. Why? Because the blood liquefies, whenever it is brought. A person I know, not knowing the prohibition, brought in a portion, and the Priest suddenly said, who showed the blood, "Who has got the Holy Cross about him?" I tell you what was told me by a grave and religious man. It is a curious coincidence that in telling this to our Father Director here, he said, "Why, we have a portion of St. Pantaleon's blood at the Chiesa Nuova, and it is always liquid."'

After leaving Naples, Newman visited Loreto, and inspected the house of the Holy Family, which, as is known to the faithful, was transported thither, in three hops, from Palestine.

'I went to Loreto,' he wrote, 'with a simple faith, believing what I still more believed when I saw it. I have no doubt now. If you ask me why I believe it, it is because everyone believes it at Rome; cautious as they are and sceptical about some other things. I have no antecedent difficulty in the matter. He who floated the Ark on the surges of a world-wide sea, and enclosed in it all living things, who has hidden the terrestrial paradise, who said that faith might move mountains, who sustained thousands for forty years in a sterile wilderness, who transported Elias and keeps him hidden till the end, could do this wonder also.'

Here, whatever else there may be, there is certainly no trace of a desire to deceive. Could a state of mind, in fact, be revealed with more absolute transparency?

When Newman was a child he 'wished that he could believe the Arabian Nights were true'. When he came to be a man, his wish seems to have been granted.

Tract No. 90 was officially condemned by the authorities at Oxford, and in the hubbub that followed, the contending parties closed their ranks; henceforward, any compromise between the friends and the enemies of the Movement was impossible. Archdeacon Manning was in too conspicuous a position to be able to remain silent; he was obliged to declare himself, and he did not hesitate. In an archidiaconal charge, delivered within a few months of his appointment, he firmly repudiated the Tractarians. But the repudiation was not deemed sufficient, and a year later he repeated it with greater emphasis. Still, however, the horrid rumours were afloat. The "Record" began to investigate matters, and its vigilance was soon rewarded by an alarming discovery: the sacrament had been administered in Chichester Cathedral on a weekday, and 'Archdeacon Manning, one of the most noted and determined of the Tractarians, had acted a conspicuous part on the occasion'. It was clear that the only way of silencing these malevolent whispers was by some public demonstration whose import nobody could doubt. The annual sermon preached on Guy Fawkes Day before the University of Oxford seemed to offer the very opportunity that Manning required. He seized it; got himself appointed preacher; and delivered from the pulpit of St. Mary's a virulently Protestant harangue. This time there could indeed be no doubt about the matter: Manning had shouted 'No Popery!' in the very citadel of the Movement, and every one, including Newman, recognised that he had finally cut himself off from his old friends. Everyone, that is to say, except the Archdeacon himself. On the day after the sermon, Manning walked out to the neighbouring village of Littlemore, where Newman was now living in retirement with a few chosen disciples, in the hope of being able to give a satisfactory explanation of what he had done. But he was disappointed; for when, after an awkward interval, one of the disciples appeared at the door, he was informed that Mr. Newman was not at home.

With his retirement to Littlemore, Newman had entered upon the final period of his Anglican career. Even he could no longer help perceiving that the end was now only a matter of time. His progress was hastened in an agitating manner by the indiscreet activity of one of his proselytes, W. G. Ward. a young man who combined an extraordinary aptitude for a priori reasoning with a passionate devotion to Opera Bouffe. It was difficult, in fact, to decide whether the inner nature of Ward was more truly expressing itself when he was firing off some train of scholastic paradoxes on the Eucharist or when he was trilling the airs of Figaro and plunging through the hilarious roulades of the Largo al Factotum. Even Dr. Pusey could not be quite sure, though he was Ward's spiritual director. On one occasion his young penitent came to him, and confessed that a vow which he had taken to abstain from music during Lent was beginning to affect his health. Could Dr. Pusey see his way to releasing him from the vow? The Doctor decided that a little sacred music would not be amiss. Ward was all gratitude, and that night a party was arranged in a friend's rooms. The concert began with the solemn harmonies of Handel, which were followed by the holy strains of the 'Oh Salutaris' of Cherubini. Then came the elevation and the pomp of 'Possenti Numi' from the Magic Flute. But, alas! there lies much danger in Mozart. The page was turned and there was the delicious duet between Papageno and Papagena. Flesh and blood could not resist that; then song followed song, the music waxed faster and lighter, until, at last Ward burst into the intoxicating merriment of the Largo al Factotum. When it was over, a faint but persistent knocking made itself heard upon the wall; and it was only then that the company remembered that the rooms next door were Dr. Pusey's.

The same entrainment which carried Ward away when he sat down to a piano possessed him whenever he embarked on a religious discussion. 'The thing that was utterly abhorrent to him,' said one of his friends, 'was to stop short.' Given the premises, he would follow out their implications with the mercilessness of a medieval monk, and when he had reached the last limits of argument, be ready to maintain whatever propositions he might find there with his dying breath. He had the extreme innocence of a child and a mathematician. Captivated by the glittering eye of Newman, he swallowed whole the supernatural conception of the universe which Newman had evolved, accepted it as a fundamental premise, and 'began at once to deduce from it whatsoever there might be to be deduced.' His very first deductions included irrefutable proofs of (I) God's particular providence for individuals; (2) the real efficacy of intercessory prayer; (3) the reality of our communion with the saints departed; (4) the constant presence and assistance of the angels of God. Later on he explained mathematically the importance of the Ember Days: 'Who can tell,' he added, 'the degree of blessing lost to us in this land by neglecting, as we alone of Christian Churches do neglect, these holy days?' He then proceeded to convict the Reformers, not only of rebellion, but'—for my own part I see not how we can avoid adding—of perjury.' Every day his arguments became more extreme, more rigorously exact, and more distressing to his master. Newman was in the position of a cautious commander-in-chief being hurried into an engagement against his will by a dashing cavalry officer. Ward forced him forward step by step towards-no! he could not bear it; he shuddered and drew back. But it was of no avail. In vain did Keble and Pusey wring their hands and stretch forth their pleading arms to their now vanishing brother. The fatal moment was fast approaching. Ward at last published a devastating book in which he proved conclusively, by a series of syllogisms, that the only proper course for the Church of England was to repent in sackcloth and ashes her separation from the Communion of Rome. The reckless author was deprived of his degree by an outraged University, and a few weeks later was received into the Catholic Church.

Newman, in a kind of despair, had flung himself into the labours of historical compilation. His views of history had changed since the days when, as an undergraduate, he had feasted on the worldly pages of Gibbon.

'Revealed religion,' he now thought, 'furnishes facts to other sciences, which those sciences, left to themselves, would never reach. Thus, in the science of history, the preservation of our race in Noah's Ark is an historical fact, which history never would arrive at without revelation.'

With these principles to guide him, he plunged with his disciples into a prolonged study of the English Saints. Biographies soon appeared of St. Bega, St. Adamnan, St. Gundleus, St. Guthlake, Brother Drithelm, St. Amphibalus, St. Wuistan, St. Ebba, St. Neot, St. Ninian, and Cunibert the Hermit. Their austerities, their virginity, and their miraculous powers were described in detail. The public learned with astonishment that St Ninian had turned a staff into a tree; that St. German had stopped a cock from crowing, and that a child had been raised from the dead to convert St. Helier. The series has subsequently been continued by a more modern writer whose relation of the history of the blessed St. Mael contains, perhaps, even more matter for edification than Newman's biographies.

At the time, indeed, those works caused considerable scandal. Clergymen denounced them in pamphlets. St. Cuthbert was described by his biographer as having 'carried the jealousy of women, characteristic of all the saints, to an extraordinary pitch'. An example was given, whenever he held a spiritual conversation with St Ebba, he was careful to spend the ensuing ours of darkness 'in prayer, up to his neck in water'. 'Persons who invent such tales,' wrote one indignant commentator, 'cast very grave and just suspicions on the purity of their own minds. And young persons, who talk and think in this way, are in extreme danger of falling into sinful habits. As to the volumes before us, the authors have, in their fanatical panegyrics of virginity, made use of language downright profane.'

One of the disciples at Littlemore was James Anthony Froude, the younger brother of Hurrell, and it fell to his lot to be responsible for the biography of St. Neot. While he was composing it, he began to feel some qualms. Saints who lighted fires with icicles, changed bandits into wolves, and floated across the Irish Channel on altar-stones, produced a disturbing effect on his historical conscience. But he had promised his services to Newman, and he determined to carry through the work in the spirit in which he had begun it. He did so; but he thought it proper to add the following sentence by way of conclusion: 'This is all, and indeed rather more than all, that is known to men of the blessed St. Neot; but not more than is known to the angels in heaven.'

Meanwhile, the English Roman Catholics were growing impatient; was the great conversion never coming, for which they had prayed so fervently and so long? Dr. Wiseman, at the head of them, was watching and waiting with special eagerness. His hand was held out under the ripening fruit; the delicious morsel seemed to be trembling on its stalk; and yet it did not fall. At last, unable to bear the suspense any longer, he dispatched to Littlemore Father Smith, an old pupil of Newman's, who had lately joined the Roman communion, with instructions that he should do his best, under cover of a simple visit of friendship, to discover how the land lay. Father Smith was received somewhat coldly, and the conversation ran entirely on topics which had nothing to do with religion. When the company separated before dinner, he was beginning to think that his errand had been useless; but, on their reassembling, he suddenly noticed that Newman had changed his trousers, and that the colour of the pair which he was now wearing was grey. At the earliest moment, the emissary rushed back post-haste to Dr. Wiseman. 'All is well,' he exclaimed; 'Newman no longer considers that he is in Anglican orders." Praise be to God!' answered Dr Wiseman. 'But how do you know?' Father Smith described what he had seen. 'Oh, is that all? My dear father, how can you be so foolish?' But Father Smith was not to be shaken. 'I know the man,' he said, and I know what it means. 'Newman will come, and he will come soon.'

And Father Smith was right. A few weeks later, Newman suddenly slipped off to a priest, and all was over. Perhaps he would have hesitated longer still, if he could have foreseen how he was to pass the next thirty years of his unfortunate existence; but the future was hidden, and all that was certain was that the past had gone forever, and that his eyes would rest no more upon the snapdragons of Trinity.

The Oxford Movement was now ended. The University breathed such a sigh of relief as usually follows the difficult expulsion of a hard piece of matter from a living organism, and actually began to attend to education. As for the Church of England, she had tasted blood, and it was clear that she would never again be content with a vegetable diet. Her clergy, however, maintained their reputation for judicious compromise, for they followed Newman up to the very point beyond which his conclusions were logical, and, while they intoned, confessed, swung incense, and burned candles with the exhilaration of converts, they yet managed to do so with a subtle nuance which showed that they had nothing to do with Rome. Various individuals underwent more violent changes. Several had preceded Newman into the Roman fold; among others an unhappy Mr. Sibthorpe, who subsequently changed his mind, and returned to the Church of his fathers, and then—perhaps it was only natural—changed his mind again. Many more followed Newman, and Dr. Wiseman was particularly pleased by the conversion of a Mr. Morris, who, as he said, was 'the author of the essay, which won the prize on the best method of proving Christianity to the Hindus'. Hurrell Froude had died before Newman had read the fatal article on St. Augustine; but his brother, James Anthony, together with Arthur Clough, the poet, went through an experience which was more distressing in those days than it has since become; they lost their faith. With this difference, however, that while in Froude's case the loss of his faith turned out to be rather like the loss of a heavy portmanteau, which one afterwards discovers to have been full of old rags and brickbats, Clough was made so uneasy by the loss of his that he went on looking for it everywhere as long as he lived; but somehow he never could find it. On the other hand, Keble and Pusey continued for the rest of their lives to dance in an exemplary manner upon the tight-rope of High Anglicanism; in such an exemplary manner, indeed, that the tight-rope has its dancers still.

IV

MANNING was now thirty-eight, and it was clear that he was the rising man in the Church of England. He had many powerful connections: he was the brother-in-law of Samuel Wilberforce, who had been lately made a bishop; he was a close friend of Mr. Gladstone, who was a Cabinet Minister; and he was becoming well known in the influential circles of society in London. His talent for affairs was recognised not only in the Church, but in the world at large, and he busied himself with matters of such varied scope as National Education, the administration of the Poor Law, and the Employment of Women. Mr. Gladstone kept up an intimate correspondence with him on these and on other subjects, mingling in his letters the details of practical statesmanship with the speculations of a religious thinker. 'Sir James Graham,' he wrote, in a discussion of the bastardy clauses of the Poor Law, 'is much pleased with the tone of your two communications. He is disposed, without putting an end to the application of the workhouse test against the mother, to make the remedy against the putative father "real and effective" for expenses incurred in the workhouse. I am not enough acquainted to know whether it would be advisable to go further. You have not proposed it; and I am disposed to believe that only with a revived and improved discipline in the Church can we hope for any generally effective check upon lawless lust.' 'I agree with you EMINENTLY,' he writes, in a later letter, 'in your doctrine of FILTRATION. But it sometimes occurs to me, though the question may seem a strange one, how far was the Reformation, but especially the Continental Reformation, designed by God, in the region of final causes, for that purification of the Roman Church which it has actually realised?'

In his archdeaconry, Manning lived to the full the active life of a country clergyman. His slim, athletic figure was seen everywhere in the streets of Chichester, or on the lawns of the neighbouring rectories, or galloping over the downs in breeches and gaiters, or cutting brilliant figures on the ice. He was an excellent judge of horse-flesh, and the pair of greys which drew his hooded phaeton so swiftly through the lanes were the admiration of the county. His features were already beginning to assume their ascetic cast, but the spirit of youth had not yet fled from them, so that he seemed to combine the attractions of dignity and grace. He was a good talker, a sympathetic listener, a man who understood the difficult art of preserving all the vigour of a manly character and yet never giving offence. No wonder that his sermons drew crowds, no wonder that his spiritual advice was sought for eagerly by an ever-growing group of penitents; no wonder that men would say, when his name was mentioned, 'Oh, Manning! No power on earth can keep HIM from a bishopric!'

Such was the fair outward seeming of the Archdeacon's life; but, the inward reality was different. The more active, the more fortunate, the more full of happy promise his existence became, the more persistently was his secret imagination haunted by a dreadful vision—the lake that burneth forever with brimstone and fire. The temptations of the Evil One are many, Manning knew; and he knew also that, for him at least, the most subtle and terrible of all temptations was the temptation of worldly success. He tried to reassure himself, but it was in vain. He committed his thoughts to a diary, weighing scrupulously his every motive, examining with relentless searchings into the depths of his heart. Perhaps, after all, his longings for preferment were merely legitimatehopes for 'an elevation into a sphere of higher usefulness'. But no, there was something more than that. 'I do feel pleasure,' he noted, 'in honour, precedence, elevation, the society of great people, and all this is very shameful and mean.'

After Newman's conversion, he almost convinced himself that his 'visions of an ecclesiastical future' were justified by the role that he would play as a 'healer of the breach in the Church of England'. Mr. Gladstone agreed with him; but there was One higher than Mr. Gladstone, and did He agree?

'I am pierced by anxious thoughts. God knows what my desires have been and are, and why they are crossed.... I am flattering myself with a fancy about depth and reality.... The great question is: Is God enough for you now? And if you are as now even to the end of life, will it suffice you?... Certainly I would rather choose to be stayed on God, than to be in the thrones of the world and the Church. Nothing else will go into Eternity.'

In a moment of ambition, he had applied for the Readership of Lincoln's Inn, but, owing chiefly to the hostile influence of the Record, the appointment had gone elsewhere. A little later, a more important position was offered to him— the office of sub-almoner to the Queen, which had just been vacated by the Archbishop of York, and was almost certain to lead to a mitre. The offer threw Manning into an agony of self-examination. He drew up elaborate tables, after the manner of Robinson Crusoe, with the reasons for and against his acceptance of the post:

FOR AGAINST

1. That it comes unsought. 1. Not therefore to be accepted. Such things are trials as well as leadings.

   2. That it is honourable. 2. Being what I am, ought I

           not therefore to decline it—

           (1) as humiliation;

           (2) as revenge on myself

            for Lincoln's Inn;

(3) as a testimony?

And so on. He found in the end ten 'negative reasons', with no affirmative ones to balance them, and, after a week's deliberation, he rejected the offer.

But peace of mind was as far off from him as ever. First the bitter thought came to him that 'in all this Satan tells me I am doing it to be thought mortified and holy'; and then he was obsessed by the still bitterer feelings of ineradicable disappointment and regret. He had lost a great opportunity, and it brought him small comfort to consider that 'in the region of counsels, self-chastisement, humiliation, self-discipline, penance, and of the Cross', he had perhaps done right.

The crisis passed, but it was succeeded by a fiercer one. Manning was taken seriously ill, and became convinced that he might die at any moment. The entries in his Diary grew more elaborate than ever; his remorse for the past, his resolutions for the future, his protestations of submission to the will of God, filled page after page of parallel columns, headings and sub-headings, numbered clauses, and analytical tables. 'How do I feel about Death?' he wrote.

'Certainly great fear:

   1. Because of the uncertainty of our state before God.

   2. Because of the consciousness—

      (1) of great sins past,

      (2) of great sinfulness,

      (3) of most shallow repentance.

What shall I do?'

He decided to mortify himself, to read St Thomas Aquinas, and to make his 'night prayers forty instead of thirty minutes'. He determined during Lent 'to use no pleasant bread (except on Sundays and feasts) such as cake and sweetmeat'; but he added the proviso 'I do not include plain biscuits'. Opposite this entry appears the word 'KEPT'. And yet his back-slidings were many. Looking back over a single week, he was obliged to register 'petulance twice' and 'complacent visions'. He heard his curate being commended for bringing so many souls to God during Lent, and he 'could not bear it'; but the remorse was terrible: 'I abhorred myself on the spot, and looked upward for help.' He made out list upon list of the Almighty's special mercies towards him, and they included his creation, his regeneration, and (No. 5) 'the preservation of my life six times to my knowledge:

(1) In illness at the age of nine. (2) In the water. (3) By a runaway horse at Oxford. (4) By the same. (5) By falling nearly through the ceiling of a church. (6) Again by a fall of a horse. And I know not how often in shooting, riding, etc.'

At last he became convalescent; but the spiritual experiences of those agitated weeks left an indelible mark upon his mind, and prepared the way for the great change which was to follow.

For he had other doubts besides those which held him in torment as to his own salvation; he was in doubt about the whole framework of his faith. Newman's conversion, he found, had meant something more to him than he had first realised. It had seemed to come as a call to the redoubling of his Anglican activities; but supposing, in reality, it were a call towards something very different—towards an abandonment of those activities altogether? It might be 'a trial', or again it might be a 'leading'; how was he to judge? Already, before his illness, these doubts had begun to take possession of his mind.

'I am conscious to myself,' he wrote in his Diary, 'of an extensively changed feeling towards the Church of Rome ... The Church of England seems to me to be diseased: 1. ORGANICALLY (six sub-headings). 2. FUNCTIONALLY (seven sub-headings) ... Wherever it seems healthy, it approximates the system of Rome.'

Then thoughts of the Virgin Mary suddenly began to assail him:

(1) If John the Baptist were sanctified from the womb,

   how much more the B.V.!

(2) If Enoch and Elijah were exempted from death,

   why not the B.V. from sin?

(3) It is a strange way of loving the Son to slight

   the mother!'

The arguments seemed irresistible, and a few weeks later the following entry occurs—'Strange thoughts have visited me:

(1) I have felt that the Episcopate of the Church of England is secularised and

bound down beyond hope....

(2) I feel as if a light had fallen upon me. My feeling about the Roman Church is not intellectual. I have intellectual difficulties, but the great moral difficulties seem melting.

(3) Something keeps rising and saying, "You will end in the Roman

Church".

He noted altogether twenty-five of these 'strange thoughts'. His mind hovered anxiously round—

(1) The Incarnation,

(2) The Real Presence,

i. Regeneration,

ii. Eucharist, and

(3) The Exaltation of S. M. and Saints.

His twenty-second strange thought was as follows: 'How do I know where I may be two years hence? Where was Newman five years ago?'

It was significant, but hardly surprising, that, after his illness, Manning should have chosen to recuperate in Rome. He spent several months there, and his Diary during the whole of that period is concerned entirely with detailed descriptions of churches, ceremonies, and relics, and with minute accounts of conversations with priests and nuns. There is not a single reference either to the objects of art or to the antiquities of the place; but another omission was still more remarkable. Manning had a long interview with Pius IX, and his only record of it is contained in the bald statement: 'Audience today at the Vatican'. Precisely what passed on that occasion never transpired; all that is known is that His Holiness expressed considerable surprise on learning from the Archdeacon that the chalice was used in the Anglican Church in the administration of Communion. 'What!' he exclaimed, is the same chalice made use of by everyone?' 'I remember the pain I felt,' said Manning, long afterwards, 'at seeing how unknown we were to the Vicar of Jesus Christ. It made me feel our isolation.'

On his return to England, he took up once more the work in his Archdeaconry with what appetite he might. Ravaged by doubt, distracted by speculation, he yet managed to maintain an outward presence of unshaken calm. His only confidant was Robert Wilberforce, to whom, for the next two years, he poured forth in a series of letters, headed 'UNDER THE SEAL' to indicate that they contained the secrets of the confessional—the whole history of his spiritual perturbations. The irony of his position was singular; for, during the whole of this time, Manning was himself holding back from the Church of Rome a host of hesitating penitents by means of arguments which he was at the very moment denouncing as fallacious to his own confessor. But what else could he do? When he received, for instance, a letter such as the following from an agitated lady, what was he to say?

'MY DEAR FATHER IN CHRIST,

' … I am sure you would pity me and like to help me, if you knew the unhappy, unsettled state my mind is in, and the misery of being ENTIRELY, WHEREVER I AM, with those who look upon joining the Church of Rome as the most awful "fall" conceivable to any one, and are devoid of the smallest comprehension of how any enlightened person can do it…. My old Evangelical friends, with all my deep, deep love for them, do not succeed in shaking me in the least….

'My brother has just published a book called "Regeneration", which all my friends are reading and highly extolling; it has a very contrary effect to what he would desire on my mind. I can read and understand it all in an altogether different sense, and the facts which he quotes about the articles as drawn up in 1536, and again in 1552, and of the Irish articles of 1615 and 1634, STARTLE and SHAKE me about the Reformed Church in England far more than anything else, and have done so ever since I first saw them in Mr. Maskell's pamphlet (as quoted from Mr Dodsworth's).

'I do hope you have some time and thought to pray for me still. Mr. Galton's letters long ago grew into short formal notes, which hurt me and annoyed me particularly, and I never answered his last, so, literally, I have no one to say things to and get help from, which in one sense is a comfort when my convictions seem to be leading me on and on, and gaining strength in spite of all the dreariness of my lot.

'Do you know I can't help being very anxious and unhappy about poor Sister Harriet. I am afraid of her GOING OUT OF HER MIND. She comforts herself by an occasional outpouring of everything to me, and I had a letter this morning…. She says Sister May has promised the Vicar never to talk to her or allow her to talk on the subject with her, and I doubt whether this can be good for her, because though she has lost her faith, she says, in the Church of England, yet she never thinks of what she could have faith in, and resolutely without inquiring into the question determines not to be a Roman Catholic, so that really, you see, she is allowing her mind to run adrift and yet perfectly powerless.

'Forgive my troubling you with this letter, and believe me to be always your faithful, grateful and affectionate daughter,

'EMMA RYLE.

'P.S. I wish I could see you once more so very much.'

How was Manning, a director of souls, and a clergyman of the Church of England, to reply that in sober truth there was very little to choose between the state of mind of Sister Emma, or even of Sister Harriet, and his own? The dilemma was a grievous one: when a soldier finds himself fighting for a cause in which he has lost faith, it is treachery to stop, and it is treachery to go on.

At last, in the seclusion of his library, Manning turned in agony to those old writings which had provided Newman with so much instruction and assistance; perhaps the Fathers would do something for him as well. He ransacked the pages of St. Cyprian and St. Cyril; he went through the complete works of St. Optatus and St. Leo; he explored the vast treatises of Tertullian and Justin Martyr. He had a lamp put into his phaeton, so that he might lose no time during his long winter drives. There he sat, searching St. Chrysostom for some mitigation of his anguish, while he sped along between the hedges to distant sufferers, to whom he duly administered the sacraments according to the rites of the English Church. He hurried back to commit to his Diary the analysis of his reflections, and to describe, under the mystic formula of secrecy, the intricate workings of his conscience to Robert Wilberforce. But, alas! he was no Newman; and even the fourteen folios of St. Augustine himself, strange to say, gave him very little help.

The final propulsion was to come from an entirely different quarter. In November, 1847, the Reverend Mr. Gorham was presented by the Lord Chancellor to the living of Bramford Speke in the diocese of Exeter. The Bishop, Dr. Phillpotts, was a High Churchman, and he had reason to believe that Mr. Gorham held evangelical opinions; he therefore subjected him to an examination on doctrine, which took the form partly of a verbal interrogatory, lasting thirty-eight hours, and partly of a series of one hundred and forty-nine written questions. At the end of the examination he came to the conclusion that Mr. Gorham held heretical views on the subject of Baptismal Regeneration, and he therefore refused to institute. Mr. Gorham, thereupon, took proceedings against the Bishop in the Court of Arches. He lost his case; and he then appealed to the judicial Committee of the Privy Council.

The questions at issue were taken very seriously by a large number of persons. In the first place, there was the question of Baptismal Regeneration itself. This is by no means an easy one to disentangle; but it may be noted that the doctrine of Baptism includes: (1) God's intention, that is to say, His purpose in electing certain persons to eternal life an abstruse and greatly controverted subject, upon which the Church of England abstains from strict definition; (2) God's action, whether by means of sacraments or otherwise—concerning which the Church of England maintains the efficacy of sacraments,' but does not formally deny that grace may be given by other means, repentance and faith being present; and (3) the question whether sacramental grace is given instrumentally, by and at the moment of the act of baptism, or in consequence of an act of prevenient grace rendering the receiver worthy—that is to say, whether sacramental grace in baptism is given absolutely or conditionally.

It was over this last question that the dispute raged hottest in the Gorham Case. The High Church party, represented by Dr. Phillpotts, asserted that the mere act of baptism conferred regeneration upon the recipient and washed away his original sin. To this the Evangelicals, headed by Mr. Gorham, replied that, according to the Articles, regeneration would not follow unless baptism was RIGHTLY received. What, then, was the meaning of 'rightly'? Clearly it implied not merely lawful administration, but worthy reception; worthiness, therefore, is the essence of the sacrament; and worthiness means faith and repentance. Now, two propositions were accepted by both parties—that all infants are born in original sin, and that original sin could be washed away by baptism. But how could both these propositions be true, argued Mr. Gorham, if it was also true that faith and repentance were necessary before baptism could come into operation at all? How could an infant in arms be said to be in a state of faith and repentance? How, therefore, could its original sin be washed away by baptism? And yet, as every one agreed, washed away it was.

The only solution of the difficulty lay in the doctrine of prevenient grace; and Mr. Gorham maintained that unless God performed an act of prevenient grace by which the infant was endowed with faith and repentance, no act of baptism could be effectual; though to whom, and under what conditions, prevenient grace was given, Mr. Gorham confessed himself unable to decide. The light thrown by the Bible upon the whole matter seemed somewhat dubious, for whereas the baptism of St. Peter's disciples at Jerusalem and St. Philip's at Samaria was followed by the gift of the Spirit, in the case of Cornelius the sacrament succeeded the gift. St. Paul also was baptised; and as for the language of St. John iii 5; Rom. vi 3, 4; I Peter iii 21, it admits of more than one interpretation. There could, however, be no doubt that the Church of England assented to Dr. Phillpotts' opinion; the question was whether or not she excluded Mr. Gorham's. If it was decided that she did, it was clear that henceforward, there would be very little peace for Evangelicals within her fold.

But there was another issue, even more fundamental than that of Baptismal Regeneration itself, involved in the Gorham trial. An Act passed in 1833 had constituted the Judicial Committee of the Privy Council the supreme court of appeal for such cases; and this Committee was a body composed entirely of laymen. It was thus obvious that the Royal Supremacy was still a fact, and that a collection of lawyers appointed by the Crown had the legal right to formulate the religious doctrine of the Church of England. In 1850 their judgment was delivered; they reversed the decision of the Court of Arches, and upheld the position of Mr. Gorham. Whether his views were theologically correct or not, they said, was not their business; it was their business to decide whether the opinions under consideration were contrary or repugnant to the doctrine of the Church of England as enjoined upon the clergy by its Articles, Formularies, and Rubrics; and they had come to the conclusion that they were not. The judgement still holds good; and to this day, a clergyman of the Church of England is quite at liberty to believe that Regeneration does not invariably take place when an infant is baptised.

The blow fell upon no one with greater violence than upon Manning. Not only was the supreme efficacy of the sign of the cross upon a baby's forehead one of his favourite doctrines, but up to that moment he had been convinced that the Royal Supremacy was a mere accident—a temporary usurpation which left the spiritual dominion of the Church essentially untouched. But now the horrid reality rose up before him, crowned and triumphant; it was all too clear that an Act of Parliament, passed by Jews, Roman Catholics, and Dissenters, was the ultimate authority which decided upon the momentous niceties of the Anglican faith. Mr. Gladstone also, was deeply perturbed. It was absolutely necessary, he wrote, to 'rescue and defend the conscience of the Church from the present hideous system'. An agitation was set on foot, and several influential Anglicans, with Manning at their head, drew up and signed a formal protest against the Gorham judgment. Mr. Gladstone however, proposed another method of procedure: precipitate action, he declared, must be avoided at all costs, and he elaborated a scheme for securing procrastination, by which a covenant was to bind all those who believed that an article of the creed had been abolished by Act of Parliament to take no steps in any direction, nor to announce their intention of doing so, until a given space of time had elapsed. Mr. Gladstone was hopeful that some good might come of this—though indeed he could not be sure. 'Among others,' he wrote to Manning, 'I have consulted Robert Wilberforce and Wegg-Prosser, and they seemed inclined to favour my proposal. It might, perhaps, have kept back Lord Feilding. But he is like a cork.'

The proposal was certainly not favoured by Manning. Protests and procrastinations, approving Wegg-Prossers and cork-like Lord Feildings—all this was feeding the wind and folly; the time for action had come.

'I can no longer continue,' he wrote to Robert Wilberforce, 'under oath and subscription binding me to the Royal Supremacy in Ecclesiastical causes, being convinced:

(1) That it is a violation of the Divine Office of the Church.

(2) That it has involved the Church of England in a separation from the Universal Church, which separation I cannot clear of the character of schism.

(3) That it has thereby suspended and prevented the functions of the Church of England.'

It was in vain that Robert Wilberforce pleaded, in vain that Mr. Gladstone urged upon his mind the significance of John iii 8. ['The wind bloweth where it listeth, and thou hearest the sound thereof, but canst not tell whence it cometh, and whither it goeth; so is everyone that is born of the Spirit.']

'I admit,' Mr. Gladstone wrote, 'that the words might in some way be satisfied by supposing our Lord simply to mean "the facts of nature are unintelligible, therefore, be not afraid if revealed truths be likewise beyond the compass of the understanding"; but this seems to me a meagre meaning.'

Such considerations could hold him no longer, and Manning executed the resignation of his office and benefice before a public notary. Soon afterwards, in the little Chapel off Buckingham Palace Road, kneeling beside Mr. Gladstone, he worshipped for the last time as an Anglican. Thirty years later the Cardinal told how, just before the Communion service commenced, he turned to his friends with the words:

'I can no longer take the Communion in the Church of England.' 'I rose up, and laying my hand on Mr. Gladstone's shoulder, said "Come". It was the parting of the ways. Mr. Gladstone remained; and I went my way. Mr. Gladstone still remains where I left him.'

On April 6th, 1851, the final step was taken: Manning was received into the Roman Catholic Church. Now at last, after the long struggle, his mind was at rest.

'I know what you mean,' he wrote to Robert Wilberforce, 'by saying that one sometimes feels as if all this might turn out to be only another "Land of Shadows". I have felt it in time past, but not now. The theologia from Nice to St. Thomas Aquinas, and the undivided unity suffused throughout the world, of which the Cathedra Petri is the centre, is now 1800 years old, and mightier in every power now than ever—in intellect, in science, in separation from the world; and purer too, refined by 300 years of conflict with the modern infidel civilisation—all of this is a fact more solid than the earth.'

V.

WHEN Manning joined the Church of Rome, he acted under the combined impulse of the two dominating forces in his nature. His preoccupation with the supernatural might, alone, have been satisfied within the fold of the Anglican communion; and so might his preoccupation with himself—the one might have found vent in the elaborations of High Church ritual, and the other in the activities of a bishopric. But the two together could not be quieted so easily. The Church of England is a commodious institution; she is very anxious to please, but somehow or other, she has never managed to supply a happy home to superstitious egotists. 'What an escape for my poor soul!' Manning is said to have exclaimed when, shortly after his conversion, a mitre was going a-begging. But, in truth, Manning's 'poor soul' had scented nobler quarry. To one of his temperament, how was it possible, when once the choice was plainly put, to hesitate for a moment between the respectable dignity of an English bishop, harnessed by the secular power, with the Gorham judgment as a bit between his teeth, and the illimitable pretensions of the humblest priest of Rome?

For the moment, however, it seemed as if the Fates had at last been successful in their little game of shunting Manning. The splendid career which he had so laboriously built up from the small beginnings of his Sussex curacy was shattered—and shattered by the inevitable operation of his own essential needs. He was over forty, and he had been put back once more to the very bottom rung of the ladder—a middle-aged neophyte with, so far as could be seen, no special claim to the attention of his new superiors. The example of Newman, a far more illustrious convert, was hardly reassuring: he had been relegated to a complete obscurity, in which he was to remain until extreme old age. Why should there be anything better in store for Manning? Yet it so happened that within fourteen years of his conversion Manning was Archbishop of Westminster and the supreme ruler of the Roman Catholic community in England. This time the Fates gave up the unequal struggle; they paid over their stakes in despair, and retired from the game.

Nevertheless it is difficult to feel quite sure that Manning's plunge was as hazardous as it appeared. Certainly he was not a man who was likely to forget to look before he leaped, nor one who, if he happened to know that there was a mattress spread to receive him, would leap with less conviction. In the light of after-events, one would be glad to know what precisely passed at that mysterious interview of his with the Pope, three years before his conversion. It is at least possible that the authorities in Rome had their eye on Manning; the may well have felt that the Archdeacon of Chichester would be a great catch. What did Pio Nono say? It is easy to imagine the persuasive innocence of his Italian voice. 'Ah, dear Signor Manning, why don't you come over to us? Do you suppose that we should not look after you?'

At any rate, when he did go over, Manning was looked after very thoroughly. There was, it is true, a momentary embarrassment at the outset: it was only with the greatest difficulty that he could bring himself to abandon his faith in the validity of Anglican Orders, in which he believed 'with consciousness stronger than all reasoning'. He was convinced that he was still a priest. When the Rev. Mr. Tierney, who had received him into the Roman Catholic communion, assured him that this was not the case, he was filled with dismay and mortification. After a five hour discussion, he started to his feet in a rage. 'Then, Mr. Tierney,' he exclaimed, 'you think me insincere.'

The bitter draught was swallowed at last, and, after that, all went smoothly. Manning hastened to Rome, and was immediately placed by the Pope in the highly select Accademia Ecclesiastica, commonly known as the 'Nursery of Cardinals', for the purpose of completing his theological studies. When the course was finished, he continued, by the Pope's special request, to spend six months of every year in Rome, where he preached to the English visitors, became acquainted with the great personages of the Papal court, and enjoyed the privilege of constant interviews with the Holy Father. At the same time, he was able to make himself useful in London, where Cardinal Wiseman, the newly created Archbishop of Westminster, was seeking to reanimate the Roman Catholic community. Manning was not only extremely popular in the pulpit and in the confessional; he was not only highly efficient as a gleaner of souls—and of souls who moved in the best society; he also possessed a familiarity with official persons and official ways, which was invaluable. When the question arose of the appointment of Catholic chaplains in the Crimea during the war, it was Manning who approached the Minister, interviewed the Permanent Secretary, and finally succeeded in obtaining all that was required. When a special Reformatory for Catholic children was proposed, Manning carried through the negotiation with the Government. When an attempt was made to remove Catholic children from the Workhouses, Manning was again indispensable. No wonder Cardinal Wiseman soon determined to find some occupation of special importance for the energetic convert. He had long wished to establish a congregation of secular priests in London particularly devoted to his service, and the opportunity for the experiment had clearly now arisen. The order of the Oblates of St. Charles was founded in Bayswater, and Manning was put at its head. Unfortunately, no portion of the body of St. Charles could be obtained for the new community, but two relics of his blood were brought over to Bayswater from Milan. Almost at the same time the Pope signified his appreciation of Manning's efforts by appointing him Provost of the Chapter of Westminster—a position which placed him at the head of the Canons of the diocese.

This double promotion was the signal for the outbreak of an extraordinary internal struggle, which raged without intermission for the next seven years, and was to end only with the accession of Manning to the Archbishopric. The condition of the Roman Catholic community in England was at that time a singular one. On the one hand the old repressive laws of the seventeenth century had been repealed by liberal legislation, and on the other a large new body of distinguished converts had entered the Roman Church as a result of the Oxford Movement. It was evident that there was a 'boom' in English Catholicism, and, in 1850, Pius IX recognised the fact by dividing up the whole of England into dioceses, and placing Wiseman at the head of them as Archbishop of Westminster. Wiseman's encyclical, dated 'from without the Flaminian Gate', in which he announced the new departure, was greeted in England by a storm of indignation, culminating in the famous and furibund letter of Lord John Russell, then Prime Minister, against the insolence of the 'Papal Aggression'. Though the particular point against which the outcry was raised—the English territorial titles of the new Roman bishops—was an insignificant one, the instinct of Lord John and of the English people was in reality sound enough. Wiseman's installation did mean, in fact, a new move in the Papal game; it meant an advance, if not an aggression—a quickening in England of the long-dormant energies of the Roman Church. That Church has never had the reputation of being an institution to be trifled with; and, in those days, the Pope was still ruling as a temporal Prince over the fairest provinces of Italy. Surely, if the images of Guy Fawkes had not been garnished, on that fifth of November, with triple crowns, it would have been a very poor compliment to His Holiness.

But it was not only the honest Protestants of England who had cause to dread the arrival of the new Cardinal Archbishop; there was a party among the Catholics themselves who viewed his installation with alarm and disgust. The families in which the Catholic tradition had been handed down uninterruptedly since the days of Elizabeth, which had known the pains of exile and of martyrdom, and which clung together an alien and isolated group in the midst of English society, now began to feel that they were, after all, of small moment in the counsels of Rome. They had laboured through the heat of the day, but now it seemed as if the harvest was to be gathered in by a crowd of converts who were proclaiming on every side as something new and wonderful the truths which the Old Catholics, as they came to be called, had not only known, but for which they had suffered for generations. Cardinal Wiseman, it is true, was no convert; he belonged to one of the oldest of the Catholic families; but he had spent most of his life in Rome, he was out of touch with English traditions, and his sympathy with Newman and his followers was only too apparent. One of his first acts as Archbishop was to appoint the convert W. G. Ward, who was not even in holy orders, to be Professor of Theology at St. Edmund's College—the chief seminary for young priests, in which the ancient traditions of Douay were still flourishing. Ward was an ardent Papalist and his appointment indicated clearly enough that in Wiseman's opinion there was too little of the Italian spirit in the English community. The uneasiness of the Old Catholics was becoming intense, when they were reassured by Wiseman's appointing as his co-adjutor and successor his intimate friend, Dr. Errington, who was created on the occasion Archbishop of Trebizond in partibus infidelium. Not only was Dr. Errington an Old Catholic of the most rigid type, he was a man of extreme energy, whose influence was certain to be great; and, in any case, Wiseman was growing old, so that before very long it seemed inevitable that the policy of the diocese would be in proper hands. Such was the position of affairs when, two years after Errington's appointment, Manning became head of the Oblates of St. Charles and Provost of the Chapter of Westminster.

The Archbishop of Trebizond had been for some time growing more and more suspicious of Manning's influence, and this sudden elevation appeared to justify his worst fears. But his alarm was turned to fury when he learned that St. Edmund's College, from which he had just succeeded in removing the obnoxious W. G. Ward, was to be placed under the control of the Oblates of St. Charles. The Oblates did not attempt to conceal the fact that one of their principal aims was to introduce the customs of a Roman Seminary into England. A grim perspective of espionage and tale-bearing, foreign habits, and Italian devotions opened out before the dismayed eyes of the Old Catholics; they determined to resist to the utmost; and it was upon the question of the control of St. Edmund's that the first battle in the long campaign between Errington and Manning was fought.

Cardinal Wiseman was now obviously declining towards the grave. A man of vast physique—'your immense', an Irish servant used respectfully to call him —of sanguine temperament, of genial disposition, of versatile capacity, he seemed to have engrafted upon the robustness of his English nature the facile, child-like, and expansive qualities of the South. So far from being a Bishop Blougram (as the rumour went) he was, in fact, the very antithesis of that subtle and worldly-wise ecclesiastic. He had innocently looked forward all his life to the reunion of England to the See of Peter, and eventually had come to believe that, in God's hand, he was the instrument destined to bring about this miraculous consummation. Was not the Oxford Movement, with its flood of converts, a clear sign of the Divine will? Had he not himself been the author of that momentous article on St. Augustine and the Donatists, which had finally convinced Newman that the Church of England was in schism? And then, had he not been able to set afoot a Crusade of Prayer throughout Catholic Europe for the conversion of England?

He awaited the result with eager expectation, and in the meantime he set himself to smooth away the hostility of his countrymen by delivering courses of popular lectures on literature and archaeology. He devoted much time and attention to the ceremonial details of his princely office. His knowledge of rubric and ritual, and of the symbolical significations of vestments, has rarely been equalled, and he took a profound delight in the ordering and the performance of elaborate processions. During one of these functions, an unexpected difficulty arose: the Master of Ceremonies suddenly gave the word for a halt, and, on being asked the reason, replied that he had been instructed that moment by special revelation to stop the procession. The Cardinal, however, was not at a loss. 'You may let the procession go on,' he smilingly replied. 'I have just obtained permission, by special revelation, to proceed with it.' His leisure hours he spent in the writing of edifying novels, the composition of acrostics in Latin Verse, and in playing battledore and shuttlecock with his little nieces. There was, indeed, only one point in which he resembled Bishop Blougram—his love of a good table. Some of Newman's disciples were astonished and grieved to find that he sat down to four courses of fish during Lent. 'I am sorry to say,' remarked one of them afterwards, 'that there is a lobster salad side to the Cardinal.'

It was a melancholy fate which ordained that the last years of this comfortable, easygoing, innocent old man should be distracted and embittered by the fury of opposing principles and the venom of personal animosities. But so it was. He had fallen into the hands of one who cared very little for the gentle pleasures of repose. Left to himself, Wiseman might have compromised with the Old Catholics and Dr. Errington; but when Manning had once appeared upon the scene, all compromise became impossible. The late Archdeacon of Chichester, who had understood so well and practised with such careful skill the precept of the golden mean so dear to the heart of the Church of England, now, as Provost of Westminster, flung himself into the fray with that unyielding intensity of fervour, that passion for the extreme and the absolute, which is the very lifeblood of the Church of Rome. Even the redoubtable Dr. Errington, short, thickset, determined, with his `hawk-like expression of face', as a contemporary described him, 'as he looked at you through his blue spectacles', had been known to quail in the presence of his, antagonist, with his tall and graceful figure, his pale ascetic features, his compressed and icy lips, his calm and penetrating gaze. As for the poor Cardinal, he was helpless indeed.

Henceforward, there was to be no paltering with that dangerous spirit of independence—was it not almost Gallicanism which possessed the Old Catholic families of England? The supremacy of the Vicar of Christ must be maintained at all hazards. Compared with such an object, what were the claims of personal affection and domestic peace? The Cardinal pleaded in vain; his lifelong friendship with Dr. Errington was plucked up by the roots, and the harmony of his private life was utterly destroyed. His own household was turned against him. His favourite nephew, whom he had placed among the Oblates under Manning's special care, left the congregation and openly joined the party of Dr. Errington. His secretary followed suit; but saddest of all was the case of Monsignor Searle. Monsignor Searle, in the capacity of confidential man of affairs, had dominated over the Cardinal in private for years with the autocratic fidelity of a servant who has grown indispensable. His devotion, in fact, seemed to have taken the form of physical imitation, for he was hardly less gigantic than his master. The two were inseparable; their huge figures loomed together like neighbouring mountains; and on one occasion, meeting them in the street, a gentleman congratulated Wiseman on 'your Eminence's fine son'. Yet now even this companionship was broken up. The relentless Provost here too brought a sword. There were explosions and recriminations. Monsignor Searle, finding that his power was slipping from him, made scenes and protests, and at last was foolish enough to accuse Manning of peculation to his face; after that it was clear that his day was over; he was forced to slink snarling into the background, while the Cardinal shuddered through all his immensity, and wished many times that he were already dead.

Yet, he was not altogether without his consolations; Manning took care to see to that. His piercing eye had detected the secret way into the recesses of the Cardinal's heart—had discerned the core of simple faith which underlay that jovial manner and that facile talk. Others were content to laugh and chatter and transact their business; Manning was more artistic. He watched his opportunity, and then, when the moment came, touched with a deft finger the chord of the Conversion of England. There was an immediate response, and he struck the same chord again, and yet again. He became the repository of the Cardinal's most intimate aspirations. He alone sympathised and understood. 'If God gives me strength to undertake a great wrestling-match with infidelity,' Wiseman wrote, 'I shall owe it to him.'

But what he really found himself undertaking was a wrestling-match with Dr. Errington. The struggle over St. Edmund's College grew more and more acute. There were high words in the Chapter, where Monsignor Searle led the assault against the Provost, and carried a resolution declaring that the Oblates of St. Charles had intruded themselves illegally into the Seminary. The Cardinal quashed the proceedings of the Chapter; whereupon, the Chapter appealed to Rome. Dr. Errington, carried away by the fury of the controversy, then appeared as the avowed opponent of the Provost and the Cardinal. With his own hand he drew up a document justifying the appeal of the Chapter to Rome by Canon Law and the decrees of the Council of Trent. Wiseman was deeply pained: 'My own co-adjutor,' he exclaimed, 'is acting as solicitor against me in a lawsuit.' There was a rush to Rome, where, for several ensuing years, the hostile English parties were to wage a furious battle in the antechambers of the Vatican. But the dispute over the Oblates now sank into insignificance beside the rage of contention which centred round a new and far more deadly question; for the position of Dr. Errington himself was at stake. The Cardinal, in spite of illness, indolence, and the ties of friendship, had been brought at last to an extraordinary step—he was petitioning the Pope for nothing less than the deprivation and removal of the Archbishop of Trebizond.

The precise details of what followed are doubtful. It is only possible to discern with clearness, amid a vast cloud of official documents and unofficial correspondences in English, Italian, and Latin, of Papal decrees and voluminous scritture, of confidential reports of episcopal whispers and the secret agitations of Cardinals, the form of Manning, restless and indomitable, scouring like a stormy petrel the angry ocean of debate. Wiseman, dilatory, unbusinesslike, and infirm, was ready enough to leave the conduct of affairs in his hands. Nor was it long before Manning saw where the key of the whole position lay. As in the old days, at Chichester, he had secured the goodwill of Bishop Shuttleworth by cultivating the friendship of Archdeacon Hare, so now, on this vaster scale of operations, his sagacity led him swiftly and unerringly up the little winding staircase in the Vatican and through the humble door which opened into the cabinet of Monsignor Talbot, the private secretary of the Pope. Monsignor Talbot was a priest who embodied in a singular manner, if not the highest, at least the most persistent traditions of the Roman Curia. He was a master of various arts which the practice of ages has brought to perfection under the friendly shadow of the triple tiara. He could mingle together astuteness and holiness without any difficulty; he could make innuendoes as naturally as an ordinary man makes statements of fact; he could apply flattery with so unsparing a hand that even Princes of the Church found it sufficient; and, on occasion, he could ring the changes of torture on a human soul with a tact which called forth universal approbation. With such accomplishments, it could hardly be expected that Monsignor Talbot should be remarkable either for a delicate sense of conscientiousness or for an extreme refinement of feeling, but then it was not for those qualities that Manning was in search when he went up the winding stair. He was looking for the man who had the ear of Pio Nono; and, on the other side of the low-arched door, he found him. Then he put forth all his efforts; his success was complete; and an alliance began which was destined to have the profoundest effect upon Manning's career, and was only dissolved when, many years later, Monsignor Talbot was unfortunately obliged to exchange his apartment in the Vatican for a private lunatic asylum at Passy.

It was determined that the coalition should be ratified by the ruin of Dr. Errington. When the moment of crisis was seen to be approaching, Wiseman was summoned to Rome, where he began to draw up an immense scrittura containing his statement of the case. For months past, the redoubtable energies of the Archbishop of Trebizond had been absorbed in a similar task. Folio was being piled upon folio, when a sudden blow threatened to put an end to the whole proceeding in a summary manner. The Cardinal was seized by violent illness, and appeared to be upon his deathbed. Manning thought for a moment that his labours had been in vain and that all was lost. But the Cardinal recovered; Monsignor Talbot used his influence as he alone knew how; and a papal decree was issued by which Dr. Errington was 'liberated' from the Coadjutorship of Westminster, together with the right of succession to the See.

It was a supreme act of authority—a 'colpo di stato di Dominiddio', as the Pope himself said—and the blow to the Old Catholics was correspondingly severe. They found themselves deprived at one fell swoop both of the influence of their most energetic supporter and of the certainty of coming into power at Wiseman's death. And in the meantime, Manning was redoubling his energies at Bayswater. Though his Oblates had been checked over St. Edmund's, there was still no lack of work for them to do. There were missions to be carried on, schools to be managed, funds to be collected. Several new churches were built; a community of most edifying nuns of the Third Order of St. Francis was established; and L30,000, raised from Manning's private resources and from those of his friends, was spent in three years. 'I hate that man,' one of the Old Catholics exclaimed, 'he is such a forward piece.' The words were reported to Manning, who shrugged his shoulders.

'Poor man,' he said, 'what is he made of? Does he suppose, in his foolishness, that after working day and night for twenty years in heresy and schism, on becoming a Catholic, I should sit in an easy-chair and fold my hands all the rest of my life?'

But his secret thoughts were of a different caste.

'I am conscious of a desire,' he wrote in his Diary, 'to be in such a position: (I) as I had in times past; (2) as my present circumstances imply; (3) as my friends think me fit for; and (4) as I feel my own faculties tend to.

'But, God being my helper, I will not seek it by the lifting of a finger or the speaking, of a word.'

So Manning wrote, and thought, and prayed; but what are words, and thoughts, and even prayers, to the mysterious and relentless powers of circumstance and character? Cardinal Wiseman was slowly dying; the tiller of the Church was slipping from his feeble hand; and Manning was beside him, the one man with the energy, the ability, the courage, and the conviction to steer the ship upon her course. More than that; there was the sinister figure of a Dr. Errington crouching close at hand, ready to seize the helm and make straight—who could doubt it?—for the rocks. In such a situation the voice of self-abnegation must needs grow still and small indeed. Yet it spoke on, for it was one of the paradoxes in Manning's soul that that voice was never silent. Whatever else he was, he was not unscrupulous. Rather, his scruples deepened with his desires; and he could satisfy his most exorbitant ambitions in a profundity of self-abasement. And so now he vowed to Heaven that he would SEEK nothing—no, not by the lifting of a finger or the speaking of a word.

But, if something came to him—? He had vowed not to seek; he had not vowed not to take. Might it not be his plain duty to take? Might it not be the will of God?

Something, of course, did come to him, though it seemed for a moment that it would elude his grasp. Wiseman died, and there ensued in Rome a crisis of extraordinary intensity. 'Since the creation of the hierarchy,' Monsignor Talbot wrote, it is the greatest moment for the Church that I have yet seen.' It was the duty of the Chapter of Westminster to nominate three candidates for succession to the Archbishopric; they made one last effort, and had the temerity to place upon the list, besides the names of two Old Catholic bishops, that of Dr. Errington. It was a fatal blunder. Pius IX was furious; the Chapter had committed an 'insulta al Papa', he exclaimed, striking his breast three times in his rage. 'It was the Chapter that did it,' said Manning, afterwards; but even after the Chapter's indiscretion, the fatal decision hung in the balance for weeks.

'The great point of anxiety with me, wrote Monsignor Talbot to Manning, 'is whether a Congregation will be held, or whether the Holy Father will perform a Pontifical act. He himself is doubting. I therefore say mass and pray every morning that he may have the courage to choose for himself, instead of submitting the matter to a Congregation. Although the Cardinals are determined to reject Dr. Errington, nevertheless I am afraid that they should select one of the others. You know very well that Congregations are guided by the documents that are placed before them; it is for this reason that I should prefer the Pope's acting himself.'

But the Holy Father himself was doubting. In his indecision, he ordered a month of prayers and masses. The suspense grew and grew. Everything seemed against Manning. The whole English episcopate was opposed to him; he had quarrelled with the Chapter; he was a convert of but few years' standing; even the congregated Cardinals did not venture to suggest the appointment of such a man. But suddenly, the Holy Father's doubts came to an end. He heard a voice—a mysterious inward voice—whispering something in his ear. 'Mettetelo li! Mettetelo li!' the voice repeated, over and over again. Mettetelo li! It was an inspiration; and Pius IX, brushing aside the recommendations of the Chapter and the deliberations of the Cardinals, made Manning, by a Pontifical act, Archbishop of Westminster.

Monsignor Talbot's felicity was complete, and he took occasion in conveying his congratulations to his friend, to make some illuminating reflections upon the great event.

'MY policy throughout,' he wrote, 'was never to propose you DIRECTLY to the Pope, but, to make others do so, so that both you and I can always say that it was not I who induced the Holy Father to name you—which would lessen the weight of your appointment. This I say, because many have said that your being named was all my doing. I do not say that the Pope did not know that I thought you the only man eligible—as I took care to tell him over and over again what was against all the other candidates—and in consequence, he was almost driven into naming you. After he had named you, the Holy Father said to me, "What a diplomatist you are, to make what you wished come to pass!"

'Nevertheless,' concluded Monsignor Talbot, 'I believe your appointment was specially directed by the Holy Ghost.'

Manning himself was apparently of the same opinion.

'My dear Child,' he wrote to a lady penitent, 'I have in these last three weeks felt as if our Lord had called me by name. Everything else has passed out of my mind. The firm belief that I have long had that the Holy Father is the most supernatural person I have ever seen has given me this feeling more deeply. 'Still, I feel as if I had been brought, contrary to all human wills, by the Divine Will, into an immediate relation to our Divine Lord.'

'If indeed,' he wrote to Lady Herbert, 'it were the will of our Divine Lord to lay upon me this heavy burden, He could have done it in no way more strengthening and consoling to me. To receive it from the hands of His Vicar, and from Pius IX, and after long invocation of the Holy Ghost, and not only without human influences, but in spite of manifold aria powerful human opposition, gives me the last strength for such a cross.'

<h1 style="text-align:center">VI</h1>

MANNING'S appointment filled his opponents with alarm. Wrath and vengeance seemed to be hanging over them; what might not be expected from the formidable enemy against whom they had struggled for so long, and who now stood among them armed with archiepiscopal powers and invested with the special confidence of Rome? Great was their amazement, great was their relief, when they found that their dreaded master breathed nothing but kindness, gentleness, and conciliation. The old scores, they found, were not to be paid off, but to be wiped out. The new archbishop poured forth upon every side all the tact, all the courtesy, all the dignified graces of a Christian magnanimity. It was impossible to withstand such treatment. Bishops who had spent years in thwarting him became his devoted adherents; even the Chapter of Westminster forgot its hatred. Monsignor Talbot was extremely surprised. 'Your greatest enemies have entirely come round,' he wrote. 'I received the other day a panegyric of you from Searle. This change of feeling I cannot attribute to anything but the Holy Ghost.' Monsignor Talbot was very fond of the Holy Ghost; but, so far, at any rate as Searle was concerned, there was another explanation. Manning, instead of dismissing Searle from his position of 'oeconomus' in the episcopal household, had kept him on—at an increased salary; and the poor man, who had not scrupled in the days of his pride to call Manning a thief, was now duly grateful.

As to Dr. Errington, he gave an example of humility and submission by at once withdrawing into a complete obscurity. For years the Archbishop of Trebizond, the ejected heir to the See of Westminster, laboured as a parish priest in the Isle of Man. He nursed no resentment in his heart, and, after a long and edifying life of peace and silence, he died in 1886, a professor of theology at Clifton.

It might be supposed that Manning could now feel that his triumph was complete. His position was secure; his power was absolute; his prestige was daily growing. Yet there was something that irked him still. As he cast his eyes over the Roman Catholic community in England, he was aware of one figure which, by virtue of a peculiar eminence, seemed to challenge the supremacy of his own. That figure was Newman's.

Since his conversion, Newman's life had been a long series of misfortunes and disappointments. When he had left the Church of England, he was its most distinguished, its most revered member, whose words, however strange, were listened to with profound attention, and whose opinions, however dubious, were followed in all their fluctuations with an eager and indeed a trembling respect. He entered the Church of Rome, and found himself forthwith an unimportant man. He was received at the Papal Court with a politeness which only faintly concealed a total lack of interest and understanding. His delicate mind, with its refinements, its hesitations, its complexities—his soft, spectacled, Oxford manner, with its half-effeminate diffidence-such things were ill calculated to impress a throng of busy Cardinals and Bishops, whose days were spent amid the practical details of ecclesiastical organisation, the long-drawn involutions of papal diplomacy, and the delicious bickerings of personal intrigue. And when, at last, he did succeed in making some impression upon these surroundings, it was no better; it was worse. An uneasy suspicion gradually arose; it began to dawn upon the Roman authorities that Dr. Newman was a man of ideas. Was it possible that Dr. Newman did not understand that ideas in Rome were, to say the least of it, out of place? Apparently, he did not—nor was that all; not content with having ideas, he positively seemed anxious to spread them. When that was known, the politeness in high places was seen to be wearing decidedly thin. His Holiness, who on Newman's arrival had graciously expressed the wish to see him 'again and again', now, apparently, was constantly engaged. At first Newman supposed that the growing coolness was the result of misapprehension; his

Italian was faulty, Latin was not spoken at Rome, his writings had only appeared in garbled translations. And even Englishmen had sometimes found his arguments difficult to follow. He therefore determined to take the utmost care to make his views quite clear; his opinions upon religious probability, his distinction between demonstrative and circumstantial evidence, his theory of the development of doctrine and the aspects of ideas—these and many other matters, upon which he had written so much, he would now explain in the simplest language. He would show that there was nothing dangerous in what he held, that there was a passage in De Lugo which supported him—that Perrone, by maintaining that the Immaculate Conception could be defined, had implicitly admitted one of his main positions, and that his language about Faith had been confused, quite erroneously, with the fideism of M. Bautain.

Cardinal Barnabo, Cardinal Reisach, Cardinal Antonelli, looked at him with their shrewd eyes and hard faces, while he poured into their ears which, as he had already noticed with distress, were large and not too clean—his careful disquisitions; but, it was all in vain—they had clearly never read De Lugo or Perrone, and as for M. Bautain, they had never heard of him. Newman, in despair, fell back upon St. Thomas Aquinas; but, to his horror, he observed that St. Thomas himself did not mean very much to the Cardinals. With a sinking heart, he realised at last the painful truth: it was not the nature of his views, it was his having views at all, that was objectionable. He had hoped to devote the rest of his life to the teaching of Theology; but what sort of Theology could he teach which would be acceptable to such superiors? He left Rome, and settled down in Birmingham as the head of a small community of Oratorians. He did not complain; it was God's will; it was better so. He would watch and pray.

But God's will was not quite so simple as that. Was it right, after all, that a man with Newman's intellectual gifts, his devoted ardour, his personal celebrity, should sink away out of sight and use in the dim recesses of the Oratory at Birmingham? If the call were to come to him to take his talent out of the napkin, how could he refuse? And the call did come. A Catholic University was being started in Ireland and Dr. Cullen, the Archbishop of Armagh, begged Newman to become the Rector. At first he hesitated, but when he learned that it was the Holy Father's wish that he should take up the work, he could doubt no longer; the offer was sent from Heaven. The difficulties before him were very great; not only had a new University to be called up out of the void, but the position was complicated by the presence of a rival institution—the undenominational Queen's Colleges, founded by Peel a few years earlier with the object of giving Irish Catholics facilities for University education on the same terms as their fellow-countrymen. Yet Newman had the highest hopes. He dreamt of something greater than a merely Irish University—of a noble and flourishing centre of learning for the

Catholics of Ireland and England alike. And why should not his dream come true? 'In the midst of our difficulties, he said, 'I have one ground of hope, just one stay, but, as I think, a sufficient one, which serves me in the stead of all other argument whatever. It is the decision of the Holy See; St. Peter has spoken.'

The years that followed showed to what extent it was safe to depend upon St. Peter. Unforeseen obstacles cropped up on every side. Newman's energies were untiring, but so was the inertia of the Irish authorities. On his appointment, he wrote to Dr. Cullen asking that arrangements might be made for his reception in Dublin. Dr. Cullen did not reply. Newman wrote again, but still there was no answer. Weeks passed, months passed, years passed, and not a word, not a sign, came from Dr. Cullen. At last, after dangling for more than two years in the uncertainties and perplexities of so strange a situation, Newman was summoned to Dublin. There he found nothing but disorder and discouragement. The laity took no interest in the scheme; the clergy actively disliked it; Newman's authority was disregarded. He appealed to Cardinal Wiseman, and then at last a ray of hope dawned. The cardinal suggested that a bishopric should be conferred upon him, to give him a status suitable to his position; Dr. Cullen acquiesced, and Pius IX was all compliance. 'Manderemo a Newman la crocetta,' he said to Wiseman, smilingly drawing his hands down each side of his neck to his breast, 'lo faremo vescovo di Porfirio, o qualche luogo.' The news spread among Newman's friends, and congratulations began to come in. But the official intimation seemed to be unaccountably delayed; no crocetta came from Rome, and Cardinal Wiseman never again referred to the matter. Newman was left to gather that the secret representations of Dr. Cullen had brought about a change of counsel in high quarters. His pride did not allow him to inquire further; but one of his lady penitents, Miss Giberne, was less discreet. 'Holy Father,' she suddenly said to the Pope in an audience one day, 'why don't you make Father Newman a bishop?' Upon which the Holy Father looked much confused and took a great deal of snuff.

For the next five years Newman, unaided and ignored, struggled desperately, like a man in a bog, with the overmastering difficulties of his task. His mind, whose native haunt was among the far aerial boundaries of fancy and philosophy, was now clamped down under the fetters of petty detail and fed upon the mean diet of compromise and routine. He had to force himself to scrape together money, to write articles for the students' Gazette, to make plans for medical laboratories, to be ingratiating with the City Council; he was obliged to spend months travelling through the remote regions of Ireland in the company of extraordinary ecclesiastics and barbarous squireens. He was a thoroughbred harnessed to a four-wheeled cab—and he knew it. Eventually, he realised something else: he saw that the whole project of a Catholic University had been evolved as a political and ecclesiastical weapon against the Queen's

Colleges of Peel, and that was all. As an instrument of education, it was simply laughed at; and he himself had been called in because his name would be a valuable asset in a party game. When he understood that, he resigned his rectorship and returned to the Oratory.

But, his tribulations were not yet over. It seemed to be God's will that he should take part in a whole succession of schemes, which, no less than the project of the Irish University, were to end in disillusionment and failure. He was persuaded by Cardinal Wiseman to undertake the editorship of a new English version of the Scriptures, which was to be a monument of Catholic scholarship and an everlasting glory to Mother Church. He made elaborate preparations; he collected subscriptions, engaged contributors, and composed a long and learned prolegomena to the work. It was all useless; Cardinal Wiseman began to think of other things; and the scheme faded imperceptibly into thin air. Then a new task was suggested to him: "The Rambler", a Catholic periodical, had fallen on evil days; would Dr Newman come to the rescue, and accept the editorship? This time he hesitated rather longer than usual; he had burned his fingers so often—he must be specially careful now. 'I did all I could to ascertain God's Will,' he said, and he came to the conclusion that it was his duty to undertake the work. He did so, and after two numbers had appeared, Dr. Ullathorne, the Bishop of Birmingham, called upon him, and gently hinted that he had better leave the paper alone. Its tone was not liked at Rome; it had contained an article criticising St. Pius V, and, most serious of all, the orthodoxy of one of Newman's own essays had appeared to be doubtful. He resigned, and in the anguish of his heart, determined never to write again. One of his friends asked him why he was publishing nothing. 'Hannibal's elephants,' he replied, 'never could learn the goose-step.'

Newman was now an old man—he was sixty-three years of age. What had he to look forward to? A few last years of insignificance and silence. What had he to look back upon? A long chronicle of wasted efforts, disappointed hopes, neglected possibilities, unappreciated powers. And now all his labours had ended by his being accused at Rome of lack of orthodoxy. He could no longer restrain his indignation, and in a letter to one of his lady penitents, he gave vent to the bitterness of his soul. When his Rambler article had been complained of, he said, there had been some talk of calling him to Rome.

'Call me to Rome,' he burst out—'what does that mean? It means to sever an old man from his home, to subject him to intercourse with persons whose languages are strange to him—to food and to fashions which are almost starvation on the one hand, and involve restless days and nights on the other— it means to oblige him to dance attendance on Propaganda week after week and month after month—it means his death. (It was the punishment on Dr. Baines, 1840-1, to keep him at the door of Propaganda for a year.)

'This is the prospect which I cannot but feel probable, did I say anything which one Bishop in England chose to speak against and report. Others have been killed before me. Lucas went of his own accord indeed—but when he got there, oh!' How much did he, as loyal a son of the Church and the Holy See as ever was, what did he suffer because Dr. Cullen was against him? He wandered (as Dr. Cullen said in a letter he published in a sort of triumph), he wandered from Church to Church without a friend, and hardly got an audience from the Pope. 'And I too should go from St. Philip to Our Lady, and to St. Peter and St. Paul, and to St. Laurence and to St. Cecilia, and, if it happened to me as to Lucas, should come back to die.'

Yet, in spite of all, in spite of these exasperations of the flesh, these agitations of the spirit, what was there to regret? Had he not a mysterious consolation which outweighed every grief? Surely, surely, he had.

'Unveil, O Lord, and on us shine,

In glory and in grace,'

he exclaims in a poem written at this time, called 'The Two Worlds':

'This gaudy world grows pale before

The beauty of Thy face.

'Till Thou art seen it seems to he

A sort of fairy ground,

Where suns unsetting light the sky,

And flowers and fruit abound.

'But when Thy keener, purer beam

Is poured upon our sight,

It loses all its power to charm,

And what was day is night …

'And thus, when we renounce for Thee

Its restless aims and fears,

The tender memories of the past,

The hopes of coming years,

'Poor is our sacrifice, whose eyes

Are lighted from above;

We offer what we cannot keep,

What we have ceased to love.'

Such were Newman's thoughts when an unexpected event occurred which produced a profound effect upon his life: Charles Kingsley attacked his good faith, and the good faith of Catholics in general, in a magazine article. Newman protested, and Kingsley rejoined in an irate pamphlet. Newman's reply was the Apologia pro Vita Sua, which he wrote in seven weeks, sometimes working twenty-two hours at a stretch, 'constantly in tears, and constantly crying out with distress'. The success of the book, with its transparent candour, its controversial brilliance, the sweep and passion of its rhetoric, the depth of its personal feeling, was immediate and overwhelming; it was recognised at once as a classic, not only by Catholics, but by the whole English world. From every side expressions of admiration, gratitude, and devotion poured in. It was impossible for one so sensitive as Newman to the opinions of other people to resist the happy influence of such an unlooked-for, such an enormous triumph. The cloud of his dejection began to lift; et l'espoir malgre lui s'est glisse dans son coeur.

It was only natural that at such a moment his thoughts should return to Oxford. For some years past proposals had been on foot for establishing there a Hall, under Newman's leadership, for Catholic undergraduates. The scheme had been looked upon with disfavour in Rome, and it had been abandoned; but now a new opportunity presented itself—some land in a suitable position came into the market. Newman, with his reviving spirits, felt that he could not let this chance go by, and bought the land. It was his intention to build there not a Hall, but a Church, and to set on foot a 'House of the Oratory'. What possible objection could there be to such a scheme? He approached the Bishop of Birmingham, who gave his approval; in Rome itself there was no hostile sign. The laity were enthusiastic and subscriptions began to flow in. Was it possible that all was well at last? Was it conceivable that the strange and weary pilgrimage of so many years should end at length in quietude, if not in happiness, where it had begun?

It so happened that it was at this very time that Manning was appointed to the See of Westminster. The destinies of the two men, which had run parallel to one another in so strange a fashion and for so many years, were now for a moment suddenly to converge. Newly clothed with all the attributes of ecclesiastical supremacy, Manning found himself face to face with Newman, upon whose brows were glittering the fresh laurels of spiritual victory—the crown of an apostolical life. It was the meeting of the eagle and the dove. What followed showed, more clearly perhaps than any other incident in his career, the stuff that Manning was made of. Power had come to him at last; and he seized it with all the avidity of a born autocrat, whose appetite for supreme dominion had been whetted by long years of enforced abstinence and the hated simulations of submission. He was the ruler of Roman Catholic England, and he would rule. The nature of Newman's influence it was impossible for him to understand, but he saw that it existed; for twenty years he had been unable to escape the unwelcome iterations of that singular, that alien, that rival renown; and now it stood in his path, alone and inexplicable, like a defiant ghost. 'It is remarkably interesting,' he observed coldly, when somebody asked him what he thought of the Apologia: 'it is like listening to the voice of one from the dead.' And such voices, with their sepulchral echoes, are apt to be more dangerous than living ones; they attract too much attention; they must be silenced at all costs. It was the meeting of the eagle and the dove; there was a hovering, a swoop, and then the quick beak and the relentless talons did their work.

Even before his accession to the Archbishopric, Manning had scented a peculiar peril in Newman's Oxford scheme, and so soon as he came into power, he privately determined that the author of the Apologia should never be allowed to return to his old University. Nor was there any lack of excellent reasons for such a decision. Oxford was by this time a nest of liberalism; it was no fit place for Catholic youths, and they would inevitably be attracted there by the presence of Father Newman. And then, had not Father Newman's orthodoxy been impugned? Had he not been heard to express opinions of most doubtful propriety upon the question of the Temporal Power? Was it not known that he might almost be said to have an independent mind? An influence? Yes, he had an influence no doubt; but what a fatal kind of influence to which to subject the rising generation of Catholic Englishmen!

Such were the reflections which Manning was careful to pour into the receptive car of Monsignor Talbot. That useful priest, at his post of vantage in the Vatican, was more than ever the devoted servant of the new Archbishop. A league, offensive and defensive, had been established between the two friends.

'I daresay I shall have many opportunities to serve you in Rome,' wrote Monsignor Talbot modestly, 'and I do not think any support will be useless to you, especially on account of the peculiar character of the Pope, and the spirit which pervades Propaganda; therefore, I wish you to understand that a compact exists between us; if you help me, I shall help you.' And a little later he added, 'I am glad you accept the league. As I have already done for years, I shall support you, and I have a hundred ways of doing so. A word dropped at the proper occasion works wonders.'

Perhaps it was hardly necessary to remind his correspondent of that.

So far as Newman was concerned, it so fell out that Monsignor Talbot needed no prompting. During the sensation caused by the appearance of the Apologia, it had occurred to him that it would be an excellent plan to secure Newman as a preacher during Lent for the fashionable congregation which attended his church in the Piazza del Popolo; and, he had accordingly written to invite him to Rome. His letter was unfortunately not a tactful one. He assured Newman that he would find in the Piazza del Popolo 'an audience of Protestants more educated than could ever be the case in England', and 'I think myself,' he had added by way of extra inducement, 'that you will derive great benefit from visiting Rome, and showing yourself to the Ecclesiastical Authorities.' Newman smiled grimly at this; he declared to a friend that the letter was 'insolent'; and he could not resist the temptation of using his sharp pen.

'Dear Monsignor Talbot,' he wrote in reply, 'I have received your letter, inviting me to preach in your Church at Rome to an audience of Protestants more educated than could ever be the case in England.

'However, Birmingham people have souls; and I have neither taste nor talent for the sort of work which you cut out for me. And I beg to decline your offer.

I am, yours truly,

JOHN H. NEWMAN.'

Such words were not the words of wisdom. It is easy to imagine the feelings of Monsignor Talbot. 'Newman's work none here can understand,' he burst out to his friend. 'Poor man, by living almost ever since he has been a Catholic, surrounded by a set of inferior men who idolise him, I do not think he has ever acquired the Catholic instincts.' As for his views on the Temporal Power —'well, people said that he had actually sent a subscription to Garibaldi. Yes, the man was incomprehensible, heretical, dangerous; he was "uncatholic and unchristian."' Monsignor Talbot even trembled for the position of Manning in England.

'I am afraid that the old school of Catholics will rally round Newman in opposition to you and Rome. Stand firm, do not yield a bit in the line you have taken. As I have promised, I shall stand by you. You will have battles to fight because every Englishman is naturally anti-Roman. To be Roman is an effort to an Englishman an effort. Dr. Newman is more English than the English. His spirit must be crushed.'

His spirit must be crushed! Certainly there could be no doubt of that.

'What you write about Dr Newman,' Manning replied, 'is true. Whether he knows it or not, he has become the centre of those who hold low views about the Holy See, are anti-Roman, cold and silent, to say no more, about the Temporal Power; national, English, critical of Catholic devotions, and always on the lower side.... You will take care,' he concluded, 'that things are correctly known and understood where you are.'

The confederates matured their plans. While Newman was making his arrangements for the Oxford Oratory, Cardinal Reisach visited London. 'Cardinal Reisach has just left,' wrote Manning to Monsignor Talbot: 'he has seen and understands all that is going on in England.' But Newman had no suspicions. It was true that persistent rumours of his unorthodoxy and his anti-

Roman leanings had begun to float about, and these rumours had been traced to Rome. But what were rumours? Then, too, Newman found out that Cardinal Reisach had been to Oxford without his knowledge, and had inspected the land for the Oratory. That seemed odd; but all doubts were set at rest by the arrival from Propaganda of an official ratification of his scheme. There would be nothing but plain sailing now. Newman was almost happy; radiant visions came into his mind of a wonderful future in Oxford, the gradual growth of Catholic principles, the decay of liberalism, the inauguration of a second Oxford Movement, the conversion—who knows?—of Mark Pattison, the triumph of the Church.... 'Earlier failures do not matter now,' he exclaimed to a friend. 'I see that I have been reserved by God for this.'

Just then a long blue envelope was brought into the room. Newman opened it. 'All is over,' he said, 'I am not allowed to go.' The envelope contained a letter from the Bishop announcing that, together with the formal permission for an Oratory at Oxford, Propaganda had issued a secret instruction to the effect that Newman himself was by no means to reside there. If he showed signs of doing so, he was blandly and suavely ('blande suaviterque' were the words of the Latin instrument) to be prevented. And now the secret instruction had come into operation—blande suaviterque: Dr. Newman's spirit had been crushed.

His friends made some gallant efforts to retrieve the situation; but, it was in vain. Father St. John hurried to Rome and the indignant laity of England, headed by Lord Edward Howard, the guardian of the young Duke of Norfolk, seized the opportunity of a particularly virulent anonymous attack upon Newman, to send him an address in which they expressed their feeling that 'every blow that touches you inflicts a wound upon the Catholic Church in this country'. The only result was an outburst of redoubled fury upon the part of Monsignor Talbot. The address, he declared, was an insult to the Holy See. 'What is the province of the laity?' he interjected. 'To hunt, to shoot, to entertain. These matters they understand, but to meddle with ecclesiastical matters they have no right at all.' Once more he warned Manning to be careful.

'Dr. Newman is the most dangerous man in England, and you will see that he will make use of the laity against your Grace. You must not be afraid of him. It will require much prudence, but you must be firm. The Holy Father still places his confidence in you; but if you yield and do not fight the battle of the Holy See against the detestable spirit growing up in England, he will begin to regret Cardinal Wiseman, who knew how to keep the laity in order.' Manning had no thought of 'yielding'; but, he pointed out to his agitated friend that an open conflict between himself and Newman would be 'as great a scandal to the Church in England, and as great a victory to the Anglicans, as could be'. He would act quietly, and there would be no more difficulty. The Bishops were united, and the Church was sound.

On this, Monsignor Talbot hurried to Father St. John's lodgings in Rome to express his regret at the misunderstanding that had arisen, to wonder how it could possibly have occurred, and to hope that Dr. Newman might consent to be made a Protonotary Apostolic. That was all the satisfaction that Father St. John was to obtain from his visit to Rome. A few weeks later, the scheme of the Oxford Oratory was finally quashed.

When all was over, Manning thought that the time had come for a reconciliation. He made advances through a common friend; what had he done, he asked, to offend Dr. Newman? Letters passed, and, naturally enough, they only widened the breach. Newman was not the man to be polite.

'I can only repeat,' he wrote at last, 'what I said when you last heard from me. I do not know whether I am on my head or my heels when I have active relations with you. In spite of my friendly feelings, this is the judgment of my intellect.' 'Meanwhile,' he concluded, 'I propose to say seven masses for your intention amid the difficulties and anxieties of your ecclesiastical duties.'

And Manning could only return the compliment.

At about this time, the Curate of Littlemore had a singular experience. As he was passing by the Church he noticed an old man, very poorly dressed in an old grey coat with the collar turned up, leaning over the lych gate, in floods of tears. He was apparently in great trouble, and his hat was pulled down over his eyes as if he wished to hide his features. For a moment, however, he turned towards the Curate, who was suddenly struck by something familiar in the face. Could it be—? A photograph hung over the Curate's mantelpiece of the man who had made Littlemore famous by his sojourn there more than twenty years ago—he had never seen the original; but now, was it possible—? He looked again, and he could doubt no longer. It was Dr. Newman. He sprang forward, with proffers of assistance. Could he be of any use? 'Oh no, no!' was the reply. 'Oh no, no!' But the Curate felt that he could not run away and leave so eminent a character in such distress. 'Was it not Dr. Newman he had the honour of addressing?' he asked, with all the respect and sympathy at his command. 'Was there nothing that could be done?' But the old man hardly seemed to understand what was being said to him. 'Oh no, no!' he repeated, with the tears streaming down his face, 'Oh no, no!'

VII

MEANWHILE, a remarkable problem was absorbing the attention of the Catholic Church. Once more, for a moment, the eyes of all Christendom were fixed upon Rome. The temporal Power of the Pope had now almost vanished;

but, as his worldly dominions steadily diminished, the spiritual pretensions of the Holy Father no less steadily increased. For seven centuries the immaculate conception of the Virgin had been highly problematical; Pio Nono spoke, and the doctrine became an article of faith. A few years later, the Court of Rome took another step: a Syllabus Errorum was issued, in which all the favourite beliefs of the modern world—the rights of democracies, the claims of science, the sanctity of free speech, the principles of toleration—were categorically denounced, and their supporters abandoned to the Divine wrath.

Yet it was observed that the modern world proceeded as before. Something more drastic appeared to be necessary—some bold and striking measure which should concentrate the forces of the faithful, and confound their enemies. The tremendous doctrine of Papal Infallibility, beloved of all good Catholics, seemed to offer just the opening that was required. Let that doctrine be proclaimed, with the assent of the whole Church, an article of faith, and, in the face of such an affirmation, let the modern world do its worst! Accordingly, a General Council—the first to be held since the Council of Trent more than 300 years before—was summoned to the Vatican, for the purpose, so it was announced, of providing 'an adequate remedy to the disorders, intellectual and moral, of Christendom'. The programme might seem a large one, even for a General Council; but everyone knew what it meant.

Everyone, however, was not quite of one mind. There were those to whom even the mysteries of infallibility caused some searchings of heart. It was true, no doubt, that Our Lord, by saying to Peter, 'Thou art Cephas, which is by interpretation a stone', thereby endowed that Apostle with the supreme and full primacy and principality over the Universal Catholic Church; it was equally certain that Peter afterwards became the Bishop of Rome; nor could it be doubted that the Roman Pontiff was his successor. Thus it followed directly that the Roman Pontiff was the head, heart, mind, and tongue of the Catholic Church; and moreover, it was plain that when Our Lord prayed for Peter that his faith should not fail, that prayer implied the doctrine of Papal Infallibility. All these things were obvious, and yet—and yet—might not the formal declaration of such truths in the year of his grace 1870 be, to say the least of it, inopportune? Might it not come as an offence, as a scandal even, to those unacquainted with the niceties of Catholic dogma? Such were the uneasy reflections of grave and learned ecclesiastics and theologians in England, France, and Germany. Newman was more than usually upset; Monseigneur Dupanloup was disgusted; and Dr. Dollinger prepared himself for resistance. It was clear that there would be a disaffected minority at the Council.

Catholic apologists have often argued that the Pope's claim to infallibility implies no more than the necessary claim of every ruler, of every government, to the right of supreme command. In England, for instance, the Estates of the

Realm exercise an absolute authority in secular matters; no one questions this authority, no one suggests that it is absurd or exorbitant; in other words, by general consent the Estates of the Realm are, within their sphere, infallible. Why, therefore, should the Pope, within his sphere—the sphere of the Catholic Church—be denied a similar infallibility? If there is nothing monstrous in an Act of Parliament laying down what all men shall do, why should there be anything monstrous in a Papal Encyclical laying down what all men shall believe? The argument is simple; in fact, it is too simple; for it takes for granted the very question which is in dispute. Is there indeed no radical and essential distinction between supremacy and infallibility? Between the right of a Borough Council to regulate the traffic and the right of the Vicar of Christ to decide upon the qualifications for Everlasting Bliss?

There is one distinction, at any rate, which is palpable: the decisions of a supreme authority can be altered; those of an infallible authority cannot. A Borough Council may change its traffic regulations at the next meeting; but the Vicar of Christ, when in certain circumstances and with certain precautions, he has once spoken, has expressed, for all the ages, a part of the immutable, absolute, and eternal Truth. It is this that makes the papal pretensions so extraordinary and so enormous. It is also this that gives them their charm. Catholic apologists, when they try to tone down those pretensions and to explain them away, forget that it is in their very exorbitance that their fascination lies. If the Pope were indeed nothing more than a magnified Borough Councillor, we should hardly have heard so much of him. It is not because he satisfies the reason, but because he astounds it, that men abase themselves before the Vicar of Christ.

And certainly the doctrine of Papal Infallibility presents to the reason a sufficiency of stumbling-blocks. In the fourteenth century, for instance, the following case arose. John XXII asserted in his bull 'Cum inter nonnullos' that the doctrine of the poverty of Christ was heretical. Now, according to the light of reason, one of two things must follow from this—either John XXII was himself a heretic, or he was no Pope. For his predecessor, Nicholas III, had asserted in his bull 'Exiit qui seminat' that the doctrine of the poverty of Christ was the true doctrine, the denial of which was heresy. Thus if John XXII was right, Nicholas III was a heretic, and in that case Nicholas's nominations of Cardinals were void, and the conclave which elected John was illegal—so that John was no Pope, his nominations of Cardinals were void, and the whole Papal succession vitiated. On the other hand, if John was wrong—well, he was a heretic; and the same inconvenient results followed. And, in either case, what becomes of Papal Infallibility?

But such crude and fundamental questions as these were not likely to trouble the Council. The discordant minority took another line. Infallibility they admitted readily enough, the infallibility, that is to say, of the Church; what they shrank from was the pronouncement that this infallibility was concentrated in the Bishop of Rome. They would not actually deny that, as a matter of fact, it was so concentrated; but to declare that it was, to make the belief that it was an article of faith—what could be more—it was their favourite expression—more inopportune? In truth, the Gallican spirit still lingered among them. At heart, they hated the autocracy of Rome—the domination of the centralised Italian organisation over the whole vast body of the Church. They secretly hankered, even at this late hour, after some form of constitutional government, and they knew that the last faint vestige of such a dream would vanish utterly with the declaration of the infallibility of the Pope. It did not occur to them, apparently, that a constitutional Catholicism might be a contradiction in terms, and that the Catholic Church, without the absolute dominion of the Pope, might resemble the play of Hamlet without the Prince of Denmark.

Pius IX himself was troubled by doubts. 'Before I was Pope,' he observed, 'I believed in Papal Infallibility, now I feel it.' As for Manning, his certainty was no less complete than his master's. Apart from the Holy Ghost, his appointment to the See of Westminster had been due to Pio Nono's shrewd appreciation of the fact that he was the one man in England upon whose fidelity the Roman Government could absolutely rely. The voice which kept repeating 'Mettetelo li, mettetelo li' in his Holiness's ear, whether or not it was inspired by God, was certainly inspired by political sagacity. For now Manning was to show that he was not unworthy of the trust which had been reposed in him. He flew to Rome in a whirlwind of Papal enthusiasm. On the way, in Paris, he stopped for a moment to interview those two great props of French respectability, M. Guizot and M. Thiers. Both were careful not to commit themselves, but both were exceedingly polite. 'I am awaiting your Council,' said M. Guizot, 'with great anxiety. It is the last great moral power and may restore the peace of Europe.' M. Thiers delivered a brief harangue in favour of the principles of the Revolution, which, he declared, were the very marrow of all Frenchmen; yet, he added, he had always supported the Temporal Power of the Pope. 'Mais, M. Thiers,' said Manning, 'vous etes effectivement croyant.' 'En Dieu,' replied M. Thiers.

The Rome which Manning reached towards the close of 1869 was still the Rome which, for so many centuries, had been the proud and visible apex, the palpitating heart, the sacred sanctuary, of the most extraordinary mingling of spiritual and earthly powers that the world has ever known. The Pope now, it is true, ruled over little more than the City itself—the Patrimony of St. Peter— and he ruled there less by the Grace of God than by the goodwill of Napoleon III; yet he was still a sovereign Prince, and Rome was still the capital of the Papal State; she was not yet the capital of Italy. The last hour of this strange dominion had almost struck. As if she knew that her doom was upon her, the Eternal City arrayed herself to meet it in all her glory.

The whole world seemed to be gathered together within her walls. Her streets were filled with crowned heads and Princes of the Church, great ladies and great theologians, artists and friars, diplomats and newspaper reporters. Seven hundred bishops were there from all the corners of Christendom, and in all the varieties of ecclesiastical magnificence in falling lace and sweeping purple and flowing violet veils. Zouaves stood in the colonnade of St Peter's, and Papal troops were on the Quirinal. Cardinals passed, hatted and robed, in their enormous carriage of state, like mysterious painted idols. Then there was a sudden hush: the crowd grew thicker and expectation filled, the air. Yes! it was he! He was coming! The Holy Father! But first there appeared, mounted on a white mule and clothed in a magenta mantle, a grave dignitary bearing aloft a silver cross. The golden coach followed, drawn by six horses gorgeously caparisoned, and within, the smiling white-haired Pio Nono, scattering his benedictions, while the multitude fell upon its knees as one man. Such were the daily spectacles of coloured pomp and of antique solemnity, which so long as the sun was shining, at any rate—dazzled the onlooker into a happy forgetfulness of the reverse side of the Papal dispensation—the nauseating filth of the highways, the cattle stabled in the palaces of the great, and the fever flitting through the ghastly tenements of the poor.

In St. Peter's, the North Transept had been screened off; rows of wooden seats had been erected covered with Brussels carpet; and upon these seats sat each crowned with a white mitre, the 700 Bishops in Council. Here all day long rolled forth, in sonorous Latin, the interminable periods of episcopal oratory; but it was not here that the issue of the Council was determined. The assembled Fathers might talk till the marbles of St. Peter's themselves grew weary of the reverberations; the fate of the Church was decided in a very different manner—by little knots of influential persons meeting quietly of a morning in the back room of some inconspicuous lodging-house, by a sunset rendezvous in the Borghese Gardens between a Cardinal and a Diplomatist by a whispered conference in an alcove at a Princess's evening party, with the gay world chattering all about. And, of course, on such momentous occasions as these, Manning was in his element. None knew those difficult ropes better than he; none used them with a more serviceable and yet discreet alacrity. In every juncture he had the right word, or the right silence; his influence ramified in all directions, from the Pope's audience chamber to the English Cabinet. 'Il Diavolo del Concilio' his enemies called him; and he gloried in the name.

The real crux of the position was less ecclesiastical than diplomatic. The Papal Court, with its huge majority of Italian Bishops, could make sure enough, when it came to the point, of carrying its wishes through the Council; what was far more dubious was the attitude of the foreign Governments—especially those of France and England. The French Government dreaded a schism among its Catholic subjects; it disliked the prospect of an extension of the influence of the Pope over the mass of the population of France; and, since the very existence of the last remnant of the Pope's Temporal Power depended upon the French army, it was able to apply considerable pressure upon the Vatican. The interests of England were less directly involved, but it happened that at this moment Mr. Gladstone was Prime Minister, and Mr. Gladstone entertained strong views upon the Infallibility of the Pope. His opinions upon the subject were in part the outcome of his friendship with Lord Acton, a historian to whom learning and judgment had not been granted in equal proportions, and who, after years of incredible and indeed well-nigh mythical research, had come to the conclusion that the Pope could err. In this Mr. Gladstone entirely concurred, though he did not share the rest of his friend's theological opinions; for Lord Acton, while straining at the gnat of Infallibility, had swallowed the camel of the Roman Catholic Faith. 'Que diable allait-il faire dans cette galere?' one cannot help asking, as one watched that laborious and scrupulous scholar, that lifelong enthusiast for liberty, that almost hysterical reviler of priesthood and persecution, trailing his learning so discrepantly along the dusty Roman way. But, there are some who know how to wear their Rome with a difference; and Lord Acton was one of these.

He was now engaged in fluttering like a moth round the Council and in writing long letters to Mr. Gladstone, impressing upon him the gravity of the situation, and urging him to bring his influence to bear. If the Dogma were carried—he declared, no man who accepted it could remain a loyal subject and Catholics would everywhere become 'irredeemable enemies of civil and religious liberty'. In these circumstances, was it not plainly incumbent upon the English Government, involved as it was with the powerful Roman Catholic forces in Ireland, to intervene? Mr. Gladstone allowed himself to become convinced, and Lord Acton began to hope that his efforts would be successful. But, he had forgotten one element in the situation; he had reckoned without the Archbishop of Westminster. The sharp nose of Manning sniffed out the whole intrigue. Though he despised Lord Acton almost as much as he disliked him —'such men,' he said, 'are all vanity: they have the inflation of German professors, and the ruthless talk of undergraduates'—yet he realised clearly enough the danger of his correspondence with the Prime Minister, and immediately took steps to counteract it. There was a semi-official agent of the English Government in Rome, Mr. Odo Russell, and around him Manning set to work to spin his spider's web of delicate and clinging diplomacy. Preliminary politenesses were followed by long walks upon the Pincio, and the gradual interchange of more and more important and confidential communications. Soon poor Mr. Russell was little better than a fly buzzing in gossamer. And Manning was careful to see that he buzzed on the right note. In his dispatches to the Foreign Secretary, Lord Clarendon, Mr. Russell explained in detail the true nature of the Council, that it was merely a meeting of a few Roman Catholic prelates to discuss some internal matters of Church discipline, that it had no political significance whatever, that the question of Infallibility, about which there had been so much random talk, was a purely theological question, and that, whatever decision might be come to on the subject, the position of Roman Catholics throughout the world would remain unchanged.

Whether the effect of these affirmations upon Lord Clarendon was as great as Manning supposed is somewhat doubtful; but it is at any rate certain that Mr. Gladstone failed to carry the Cabinet with him; and, when at last a proposal was definitely made that the English Government should invite the Powers of Europe to intervene at the Vatican, it was rejected. Manning always believed that this was the direct result of Mr. Russell's dispatches, which had acted as an antidote to the poison of Lord Acton's letters, and thus carried the day. If that was so, the discretion of biographers has not yet entirely lifted the veil from these proceedings Manning had assuredly performed no small service for his cause. Yet his modesty would not allow him to assume for himself a credit which, after all, was due elsewhere; and when he told the story of those days, he would add, with more than wonted seriousness, 'It was by the Divine Will that the designs of His enemies were frustrated'.

Meanwhile, in the North Transept of St. Peter's a certain amount of preliminary business had been carried through. Various miscellaneous points in Christian doctrine had been satisfactorily determined. Among others, the following Canons were laid down by the Fathers: 'If anyone does not accept for sacred and canonical the whole and every part of the Books of Holy Scripture, or deny that they are divinely inspired, let him be anathema.' 'If anyone says that miracles cannot be, and therefore, the accounts of them, even those in Holy Scriptures must be assigned a place among fables and myths, or that the divine origin of the Christian religion cannot rightly be proved from them, let him be anathema.' 'If anyone says that the doctrines of the Church can ever receive a sense in accordance with the progress of science, other than that sense which the Church has understood and still understands, let him be anathema.' 'If anyone says that it is not possible, by the natural light of human reason, to acquire a certain knowledge of the One and True God, let him be anathema.' In other words, it became an article of Faith that Faith was not necessary for a true knowledge of God. Having disposed of these minor matters, the Fathers found themselves at last approaching the great question of Infallibility.

Two main issues, it soon appeared, were before them: the. Pope's infallibility was admitted, ostensibly at least, by all; what remained to be determined was: (1) whether the definition of the Pope's Infallibility was opportune, and (2) what the definition of the Pope's Infallibility was.

(1) It soon became clear that the sense of the Council was overwhelmingly in favour of a definition. The Inopportunists were a small minority; they were outvoted, and they were obliged to give way. It only remained, therefore, to come to a decision upon the second question—what the definition should actually be.

(2) It now became the object of the Inopportunists to limit the scope of the definition as much as possible, while the Infallibilists were no less eager to extend it. Now everyone, or nearly everyone, was ready to limit the Papal Infallibility to pronouncements ex cathedra—that is to say, to those made by the Pope in his capacity of Universal Doctor; but this only served to raise the ulterior, the portentous, and indeed the really crucial question—to WHICH of the Papal pronouncements ex cathedra did Infallibility adhere?

The discussions which followed were, naturally enough, numerous, complicated, and embittered, and in all of them Manning played a conspicuous part. For two months the Fathers deliberated; through fifty sessions they sought the guidance of the Holy Ghost. The wooden seats, covered though they were with Brussels carpet, grew harder and harder; and still the mitred Councillors sat on. The Pope himself began to grow impatient; for one thing, he declared, he was being ruined by the mere expense of lodging and keeping the multitude of his adherents. 'Questi infallibilisti mi faranno fallire', said his Holiness. At length it appeared that the Inopportunists were dragging out the proceedings in the hope of obtaining an indefinite postponement. Then the authorities began to act; a bishop was shouted down, and the closure was brought into operation. At this point the French Government, after long hesitation, finally decided to intervene, and Cardinal Antonelli was informed that if the Definition was proceeded with, the French troops would be withdrawn from Rome. But the astute Cardinal judged that he could safely ignore the threat. He saw that Napoleon III was tottering to his fall and would never risk an open rupture with the Vatican. Accordingly, it was determined to bring the proceedings to a close by a final vote. Already the Inopportunists, seeing that the game was up, had shaken the dust of Rome from their feet. On July 18th, 1870, the Council met for the last time. As the first of the Fathers stepped forward to declare his vote, a storm of thunder and lightning suddenly burst over St. Peter's. All through the morning the voting continued, and every vote was accompanied by a flash and a roar from heaven. Both sides, with equal justice, claimed the portent as a manifestation of the Divine Opinion. When the votes were examined, it was found that 533 were in favour of the proposed definition and two against it. Next day, war was declared between

France and Germany, and a few weeks later the French troops were withdrawn from Rome. Almost in the same moment, the successor of St. Peter had lost his Temporal Power, and gained Infallibility.

What the Council had done was merely to assent to a definition of the dogma of the Infallibility of the Roman Pontiff which Pius IX had issued, proprio motu, a few days before. The definition itself was perhaps somewhat less extreme than might have been expected. The Pope, it declared, is possessed, when he speaks ex cathedra, of 'that infallibility with which the Redeemer willed that His Church should be endowed for defining doctrine regarding faith or morals'. Thus it became a dogma of faith that a Papal definition regarding faith or morals is infallible; but beyond that, both the Holy Father and the Council maintained a judicious reserve. Over what OTHER matters besides faith and morals the Papal infallibility might or might not extend still remained in doubt. And there were further questions, no less serious, to which no decisive answer was then, or ever has been since, provided.

How was it to be determined, for instance, which particular Papal decisions did in fact come within the scope of the definition? Who was to decide what was or was not a matter of faith or morals? Or precisely WHEN the Roman Pontiff was speaking ex cathedra? Was the famous Syllabus Errorum, for example, issued ex cathedra or not? Grave theologians have never been able to make up their minds. Yet to admit doubts in such matters as these is surely dangerous. 'In duty to our supreme pastoral office,' proclaimed the Sovereign Pontiff, 'by the bowels of Christ we earnestly entreat all Christ's faithful people, and we also command them by the authority of God and our Saviour, that they study and labour to expel and eliminate errors and display the light of the purest faith.' Well might the faithful study and labour to such ends! For, while the offence remained ambiguous, there was no ambiguity about the penalty. One hair's-breadth from the unknown path of truth, one shadow of impurity in the mysterious light of faith, and there shall be anathema! anathema! anathema! When the framers of such edicts called upon the bowels of Christ to justify them, might they not have done well to have paused a little, and to have called to mind the counsel of another sovereign ruler, though a heretic—Oliver Cromwell? 'Bethink ye, bethink ye, in the bowels of Christ, that ye may be mistaken!'

One of the secondary results of the Council was the excommunication of Dr. Dollinger, and a few more of the most uncompromising of the Inopportunists. Among these, however, Lord Acton was not included. Nobody ever discovered why. Was it because he was too important for the Holy See to care to interfere with him? Or was it because he was not important enough?

Another ulterior consequence was the appearance of a pamphlet by Mr. Gladstone, entitled 'Vaticanism', in which the awful implications involved in the declaration of Infallibility were laid before the British Public. How was it possible, Mr. Gladstone asked, with all the fulminating accompaniments of his most agitated rhetoric, to depend henceforward upon the civil allegiance of Roman Catholics? To this question the words of Cardinal Antonelli to the Austrian Ambassador might have seemed a sufficient reply. 'There is a great difference,' said his Eminence, between theory and practice. No one will ever prevent the Church from proclaiming the great principles upon which its Divine fabric is based; but, as regards the application of those sacred laws, the Church, imitating the example of its Divine Founder, is inclined to take into consideration the natural weaknesses of mankind.' And, in any case, it was hard to see how the system of Faith, which had enabled Pope Gregory XIII to effect, by the hands of English Catholics, a whole series of attempts to murder Queen Elizabeth, can have been rendered a much more dangerous engine of disloyalty by the Definition of 1870. But such considerations failed to reassure Mr. Gladstone; the British Public was of a like mind; and 145,000 copies of the pamphlet were sold within two months. Various replies appeared, and Manning was not behindhand. His share in the controversy led to a curious personal encounter.

His conversion had come as a great shock to Mr. Gladstone. Manning had breathed no word of its approach to his old and intimate friend, and when the news reached him, it seemed almost an act of personal injury. 'I felt,' Mr. Gladstone said, 'as if Manning had murdered my mother by mistake.' For twelve years the two men did not meet, after which they occasionally saw each other and renewed their correspondence. This was the condition of affairs when Mr. Gladstone published his pamphlet. As soon as it appeared, Manning wrote a letter to the New York Herald, contradicting its conclusions and declaring that its publication was 'the first event that has overcast a friendship of forty-five years'. Mr. Gladstone replied to this letter in a second pamphlet. At the close of his theological arguments, he added the following passage:

'I feel it necessary, in concluding this answer, to state that Archbishop Manning has fallen into most serious inaccuracy in his letter of November 10th, wherein he describes 'my Expostulation as the first event which has overcast a friendship of forty-five years. I allude to the subject with regret; and without entering into details.'

Manning replied in a private letter:

'My dear Gladstone,' he wrote, 'you say that I am in error in stating that your former pamphlet is the first act which has overcast our friendship.

'If you refer to my act in 1851 in submitting to the Catholic Church, by which we were separated for some twelve years, I can understand it.

'If you refer to any other act either on your part or mine I am not conscious of it, and would desire to know what it may be.

'My act in 1851 may have overcast your friendship for me. It did not overcast my friendship for you, as I think the last years have shown.

'You will not, I hope, think me over-sensitive in asking for this explanation. Believe me, yours affectionately,

'H. E. M.'

'My dear Archbishop Manning,' Mr. Gladstone answered, 'it did, I confess, seem to me an astonishing error to state in public that a friendship had not been overcast for forty-five years until now, which your letter declares has been suspended as to all action for twelve …

'I wonder, too, at your forgetting that during the forty-five years I had been charged by you with doing the work of the Antichrist in regard to the Temporal Power of the Pope.

'Our differences, my dear Archbishop, are indeed profound. We refer them, I suppose, in humble silence to a Higher Power … You assured me once of your prayers at all and at the most solemn time. I received that assurance with gratitude, and still cherish it. As and when they move upwards, there is a meeting-point for those whom a chasm separates below. I remain always, affectionately yours,

'W. E. GLADSTONE.'

Speaking of this correspondence in after years, Cardinal Manning said: 'From the way in which Mr. Gladstone alluded to the overcasting of our friendship, people might have thought that I had picked his pocket.'

VIII

IN 1875, Manning's labours received their final reward: he was made a Cardinal. His long and strange career, with its high hopes, its bitter disappointments, its struggles, its renunciations, had come at last to fruition in a Princedom of the Church.

'Ask in faith and in perfect confidence,' he himself once wrote, and God will give us what we ask. You may say, "But do you mean that He will give us the very thing?" That, God has not said. God has said that He will give you whatsoever you ask; but the form in which it will come, and the time in which He will give it, He keeps in His own power. Sometimes our prayers are answered in the very things which we put from us; sometimes it may be a chastisement, or a loss, or a visitation against which our hearts rise, and we seem to see that God has not only forgotten us, but has begun to deal with us in severity. Those very things are the answers to our prayers. He knows what we desire, and He gives us the things for which we ask; but in the form which

His own Divine Wisdom sees to be best.'

There was one to whom Manning's elevation would no doubt have given a peculiar satisfaction—his old friend Monsignor Talbot. But this was not to be. That industrious worker in the cause of Rome had been removed some years previously to a sequestered home at Passy, whose padded walls were impervious to the rumours of the outer world. Pius IX had been much afflicted by this unfortunate event; he had not been able to resign himself to the loss of his secretary, and he had given orders that Monsignor Talbot's apartment in the Vatican should be preserved precisely as he had left it, in case of his return. But Monsignor Talbot never returned. Manning's feelings upon the subject appear to have been less tender than the Pope's. In all his letters, in all his papers, in all his biographical memoranda, not a word of allusion is to be found to the misfortune, nor to the death, of the most loyal of his adherents. Monsignor Talbot's name disappears suddenly and for ever—like a stone cast into the waters.

Manning was now an old man, and his outward form had assumed that appearance of austere asceticism which is, perhaps, the one thing immediately suggested by his name to the ordinary Englishman. The spare and stately form, the head—massive, emaciated, terrible—with the great nose, the glittering eyes, and the mouth drawn back and compressed into the grim rigidities of age, self-mortification, and authority—such is the vision that still lingers in the public mind—the vision which, actual and palpable like some embodied memory of the Middle Ages, used to pass and repass, less than a generation since, through the streets of London. For the activities of this extraordinary figure were great and varied. He ruled his diocese with the despotic zeal of a born administrator. He threw himself into social work of every kind; he organised charities, he lectured on temperance; he delivered innumerable sermons; he produced an unending series of devotional books. And he brooked no brother near the throne: Newman languished in Birmingham; and even the Jesuits trembled and obeyed.

Nor was it only among his own community that his energy and his experience found scope. He gradually came to play an important part in public affairs, upon questions of labour, poverty, and education. He sat on Royal Commissions and corresponded with Cabinet Ministers. At last, no philanthropic meeting at the Guildhall was considered complete without the presence of Cardinal Manning. A special degree of precedence was accorded to him. Though the rank of a Cardinal-Archbishop is officially unknown in England, his name appeared in public documents—as a token, it must be supposed, of personal consideration—above the names of peers and bishops, and immediately below that of the Prince of Wales.

In his private life he was secluded. The ambiguities of his social position, and his desire to maintain intact the peculiar eminence of his office, combined to hold him aloof from the ordinary gatherings of society, though on the rare occasions of his appearance among fashionable and exalted persons, he carried all before him. His favourite haunt was the Athenaeum Club, where he sat scanning the newspapers, or conversing with the old friends of former days. He was a member, too, of that distinguished body, the Metaphysical Society, which met once a month during the palmy years of the seventies to discuss, in strict privacy, the fundamental problems of the destiny of man.

After a comfortable dinner at the Grosvenor Hotel, the Society, which included Professor Huxley and Professor Tyndall, Mr. John Morley and Sir James Stephen, the Duke of Argyll, Lord Tennyson, and Dean Church, would gather around to hear and discuss a paper read by one of the members upon such questions as: 'What is death?' 'Is God unknowable?' or 'The nature of the Moral Principle'. Sometimes, however, the speculations of the Society ranged in other directions.

'I think the paper that interested me most of all that were ever read at our meetings,' says Sir Mountstuart Elphinstone Grant-Duff, 'was one on "Wherein consists the special beauty of imperfection and decay?" in which were propounded the questions "Are not ruins recognised and felt to be more beautiful than perfect structures? Why are they so? Ought they to be so?"

'Unfortunately, however, the answers given to these questions by the Metaphysical Society have not been recorded for the instruction of mankind.

Manning read several papers, and Professor Huxley and Mr. John Morley listened with attention while he expressed his views upon 'The Soul before and after Death', or explained why it is 'That legitimate Authority is an Evidence of Truth'. Yet, somehow or other, his Eminence never felt quite at ease in these assemblies; he was more at home with audiences of a different kind; and we must look in other directions for the free and full manifestation of his speculative gifts.

In a series of lectures, for instance, delivered in 1861—it was the first year of the unification of Italy—upon 'The Present Crisis of the Holy See, tested by prophecy', we catch some glimpses of the kind of problems which were truly congenial to his mind.

'In the following pages,' he said, 'I have endeavoured, but for so great a subject most insufficiently, to show that what is passing in our times is the prelude of the antichristian period of the final dethronement of Christendom, and of the restoration of society without God in the world.' 'My intention is,' he continued, 'to examine the present relation of the Church to the civil powers of the world by the light of a prophecy recorded by St Paul.'

This prophecy (2 Thess. ii 3 to 11) is concerned with the coming of the

Antichrist, and the greater part of the lectures is devoted to a minute examination of this subject. There is no passage in Scripture, Manning pointed out, relating to the coming of Christ more explicit and express than those foretelling Antichrist; it therefore behoved the faithful to consider the matter more fully than they are wont to do. In the first place, Antichrist is a person. 'To deny the personality of Antichrist is to deny the plain testimony of Holy Scripture.' And we must remember that 'it is a law of Holy Scripture that when persons are prophesied of, persons appear'.

Again, there was every reason to believe that Antichrist, when he did appear, would turn out to be a Jew.

'Such was the opinion of St. Irenaeus, St. Jerome, and of the author of the work De Consummatione Mundi, ascribed to St. Hippolytus, and of a writer of a Commentary on the Epistle to the Thessalonians, ascribed to St. Ambrose, of many others, who said that he will be of the tribe of Dan: as, for instance, St. Gregory the Great, Theodoret, Aretas of Caesarea, and many more. Such also is the opinion of Bellarmine, who calls it certain. Lessius affirms that the Fathers, with unanimous consent, teach as undoubted that Antichrist will be a Jew. Ribera repeats the same opinion, and adds that Aretas, St. Bede, Haymo, St. Anselm, and Rupert affirm that for this reason the tribe of Dan is not numbered among those who are sealed in the Apocalypse ... Now, I think no one can consider the dispersion and providential preservation of the Jews among all the nations of the world and the indestructible vitality of their race without believing that they are reserved for some future action of His judgment and Grace. And this is foretold again and again in the New Testament.'

'Our Lord,' continued Manning, widening the sweep of his speculations, 'has said of these latter times: "There shall arise false Christs and false prophets, insomuch as to deceive even the elect"; that is, they shall not be deceived; but those who have lost faith in the Incarnation, such as humanitarians, rationalists, and pantheists, may well be deceived by any person of great political power and success, who should restore the Jews to their own land, and people Jerusalem once more with the sons of the Patriarchs. And, there is nothing in the political aspect of the world which renders such a combination impossible; indeed, the state of Syria, and the tide of European diplomacy, which 'is continually moving eastward, render such an event within a reasonable probability.'

Then Manning threw out a bold suggestion. 'A successful medium,' he said, 'might well pass himself off by his preternatural endowments as the promised Messiahs.'

Manning went on to discuss the course of events which would lead to the final catastrophe. But this subject, he confessed, 'deals with agencies so transcendent and mysterious, that all I shall venture to do will be to sketch in outline what the broad and luminous prophecies, especially of the Book of Daniel and the Apocalypse, set forth without attempting to enter into minute details, which can only be interpreted by the event'.

While applauding his modesty, we need follow Manning no further in his commentary upon those broad and luminous works; except to observe that 'the apostasy of the City of Rome from the Vicar of Christ and its destruction by the Antichrist' was, in his opinion, certain. Nor was he without authority for this belief. For it was held by 'Malvenda, who writes expressly on the subject', and who, besides, 'states as the opinion of Ribera, Gaspar Melus, Viegas, Suarez, Bellarmine, and Bosius that Rome shall apostatise from the faith'.

IX

THE death of Pius IX brought to Manning a last flattering testimony of the confidence with which he was regarded at the Court of Rome. In one of the private consultations preceding the Conclave, a Cardinal suggested that Manning should succeed to the Papacy. He replied that he was unfit for the position, because it was essential for the interests of the Holy See that the next Pope should be an Italian. The suggestion was pressed, but Manning held firm. Thus it happened that the Triple Tiara seemed to come, for a moment, within the grasp of the late Archdeacon of Chichester; and the cautious hand refrained.

Leo XIII was elected, and there was a great change in the policy of the Vatican. Liberalism became the order of the day. And now at last the opportunity seemed ripe for an act which, in the opinion of the majority of English Catholics, had long been due—the bestowal of some mark of recognition from the Holy See upon the labours and the sanctity of Father Newman. It was felt that a Cardinal's hat was the one fitting reward for such a life, and accordingly the Duke of Norfolk, representing the Catholic laity of England, visited Manning, and suggested that he should forward the proposal to the Vatican. Manning agreed, and then there followed a curious series of incidents—the last encounter in the jarring lives of those two men. A letter was drawn up by Manning for the eye of the Pope, embodying the Duke of Norfolk's proposal; but there was an unaccountable delay in the transmission of this letter; months passed, and it had not reached the Holy Father. The whole matter would, perhaps, have dropped out of sight and been forgotten, in a way which had become customary when honours for Newman were concerned, had not the Duke of Norfolk himself, when he was next in Rome, ventured to recommend to Leo XIII that Dr. Newman should be made a Cardinal. His Holiness welcomed the proposal; but, he said, he could do nothing until he knew the views of Cardinal Manning. Thereupon, the Duke of Norfolk wrote to Manning, explaining what had occurred; shortly afterwards, Manning's letter of recommendation, after a delay of six months, reached the Pope, and the offer of a Cardinalate was immediately dispatched to Newman.

But the affair was not yet over. The offer had been made; would it be accepted? There was one difficulty in the way. Newman was now an infirm old man of seventy-eight; and it is a rule that all Cardinals who are not also diocesan Bishops or Archbishops reside, as a matter of course, at Rome. The change would have been impossible for one of his years—for one, too, whose whole life was now bound up with the Oratory at Birmingham. But, of course, there was nothing to prevent His Holiness from making an exception in Newman's case, and allowing him to end his days in England. Yet how was Newman himself to suggest this? The offer of the Hat had come to him as an almost miraculous token of renewed confidence, of ultimate reconciliation. The old, long, bitter estrangement was ended at last. 'The cloud is lifted from me for ever!' he exclaimed when the news reached him. It would be melancholy indeed if the cup were now to be once more dashed from his lips and he was obliged to refuse the signal honour. In his perplexity he went to the Bishop of Birmingham and explained the whole situation. The Bishop assured him that all would be well; that he himself would communicate with the authorities, and put the facts of the case before them. Accordingly, while Newman wrote formally refusing the Hat, on the ground of his unwillingness to leave the Oratory, the Bishop wrote two letters to Manning, one official and one private, in which the following passages occurred:

'Dr. Newman has far too humble and delicate a mind to dream of thinking or saying anything which would look like hinting at any kind of terms with the Sovereign Pontiff.... I think, however, that I ought to express my own sense of what Dr. Newman's dispositions are, and that it will be expected of me ... I am thoroughly confident that nothing stands in the way of his most grateful acceptance, except what he tells me greatly distresses him—namely, the having to leave the Oratory at a critical period of its existence, and the impossibility of his beginning a new life at his advanced age.'

And in his private letter the Bishop said:

'Dr. Newman is very much aged, and softened with age and the trials he has had, especially the loss of his two brethren, St. John and Caswall; he can never refer to these losses without weeping and becoming speechless for a time. He is very much affected by the Pope's kindness and would, I know, like to receive the great honour offered him, but feels the whole difficulty at his age of changing his life or having to leave the Oratory—which I am sure he could not do. If the Holy Father thinks well to confer on him the dignity, leaving him where he is, I know how immensely he would be gratified, and you will know how generally the conferring on him the Cardinalate will be applauded.'

These two letters, together with Newman's refusal, reached Manning as he was on the point of starting for Rome. After he had left England, the following statement appeared in "The Times":

'Pope Leo XIII has intimated his desire to raise Dr. Newman to the rank of Cardinal, but with expressions of deep respect for the Holy See, Dr. Newman has excused himself from accepting the Purple.'

When Newman's eyes fell upon the announcement, he realised at once that a secret and powerful force was working against him. He trembled, as he had so often trembled before; and certainly the danger was not imaginary. In the ordinary course of things, how could such a paragraph have been inserted without his authority? And consequently, did it not convey to the world, not only an absolute refusal which he had never intended, but a wish on his part to emphasise publicly his rejection of the proffered honour? Did it not imply that he had lightly declined a proposal for which in reality he was deeply thankful? And when the fatal paragraph was read in Rome, might it not actually lead to the offer of the Cardinalate being finally withheld?

In great agitation, Newman appealed to the Duke of Norfolk.

'As to the statement,' he wrote, 'of my refusing a Cardinal's Hat, which is in the papers, you must not believe it, for this reason:

'Of course, it implies that an offer has been made me, and I have sent an answer to it. Now I have ever understood that it is a point of propriety and honour to consider such communications sacred. This statement, therefore, cannot come from me. Nor could it come from Rome, for it was made public before my answer got to Rome.

'It could only come, then, from someone who not only read my letter, but, instead of leaving to the Pope to interpret it, took upon himself to put an interpretation upon it, and published that interpretation to the world.

'A private letter, addressed to Roman Authorities, is interpreted on its way and published in the English papers. How is it possible that anyone can have done this?'

The crushing indictment pointed straight at Manning. And it was true. Manning had done the impossible deed. Knowing what he did, with the Bishop of Birmingham's two letters in his pocket, he had put it about that Newman had refused the Hat. But a change had come over the spirit of the Holy See. Things were not as they had once been: Monsignor Talbot was at Passy, and Pio Nono was—where? The Duke of Norfolk intervened once again; Manning was profuse in his apologies for having misunderstood Newman's intentions, and hurried to the Pope to rectify the error. Without hesitation, the Sovereign Pontiff relaxed the rule of Roman residence, and Newman became a Cardinal.

He lived to enjoy his glory for more than ten years. Since he rarely left the Oratory, and since Manning never visited Birmingham, the two Cardinals met only once or twice. After one of these occasions, on returning to the Oratory, Cardinal Newman said, 'What do you think Cardinal Manning did to me? He kissed me!'

On Newman's death, Manning delivered a funeral oration, which opened thus:

'We have lost our greatest witness for the Faith, and we are all poorer and lower by the loss.

'When these tidings came to me, my first thought was this, in what way can I, once more, show my love and veneration for my brother and friend of more than sixty years?'

In private, however, the surviving Cardinal's tone was apt to be more … direct. 'Poor Newman!' he once exclaimed in a moment of genial expansion. 'Poor Newman! He was a great hater!'

X

IN that gaunt and gloomy building—more like a barracks than an Episcopal palace—Archbishop's House, Westminster, Manning's existence stretched itself out into an extreme old age. As his years increased, his activities, if that were possible, increased too. Meetings, missions, lectures, sermons, articles, interviews, letters—such things came upon him in redoubled multitudes, and were dispatched with an unrelenting zeal. But this was not all; with age, he seemed to acquire what was almost a new fervour, an unaccustomed, unexpected, freeing of the spirit, filling him with preoccupations which he had hardly felt before. 'They say I am ambitious,' he noted in his Diary, 'but do I rest in my ambition?'

No, assuredly he did not rest; but he worked now with no arriere pensee for the greater glory of God. A kind of frenzy fell upon him. Poverty, drunkenness, vice, all the horrors and terrors of our civilisation seized upon his mind, and urged him forward to new fields of action and new fields of thought. The temper of his soul assumed almost a revolutionary cast. 'I am a Mosaic Radical,' he exclaimed; and, indeed, in the exaltation of his energies, the incoherence of his conceptions, the democratic urgency of his desires, combined with his awe-inspiring aspect and his venerable age, it was easy enough to trace the mingled qualities of the patriarch, the prophet, and the demagogue. As, in his soiled and shabby garments, the old man harangued the crowds of Bermondsey or Peckham upon the virtues of Temperance, assuring them, with all the passion of conviction, as a final argument, that the majority of the Apostles were total abstainers, this Prince of the Church might have passed as a leader of the Salvation Army. His popularity was immense, reaching its height during the great Dock Strikes of 1889, when, after the victory of the men was assured, Manning was able, by his persuasive eloquence and the weight of his character, to prevent its being carried to excess. After other conciliators—among whom was the Bishop of London— had given up the task in disgust, the octogenarian Cardinal worked on with indefatigable resolution. At last, late at night, in the schools in Kirby Street, Bermondsey, he rose to address the strikers. An enthusiastic eye-witness has described the scene:

'Unaccustomed tears glistened in the eyes of his rough and work-stained hearers as the Cardinal raised his hand and solemnly urged them not to prolong one moment more than they could help the perilous uncertainty and the sufferings of their wives and children. Just above his uplifted hand was a figure of the Madonna and Child; and some among the men tell how a sudden light seemed to swim around it as the speaker pleaded for the women and children. When he sat down all in the room knew that he had won the day, and that, so far as the Strike Committee was concerned, the matter was at an end.'

In those days, there were strange visitors at the Archbishop's House. Careful priests and conscientious secretaries wondered what the world was coming to when they saw labour leaders like Mr. John Burns and Mr. Ben Tillett, and land-reformers like Mr. Henry George, being ushered into the presence of his Eminence. Even the notorious Mr. Stead appeared, and his scandalous paper with its unspeakable revelations lay upon the Cardinal's table. This proved too much for one of the faithful tonsured dependents of the place, and he ventured to expostulate with his master. But he never did so again.

When the guests were gone, and the great room was empty, the old man would draw himself nearer to the enormous fire, and review once more, for the thousandth time, the long adventure of his life. He would bring out his diaries and his memoranda, he would rearrange his notes, he would turn over again the yellow leaves of faded correspondences; seizing his pen, he would pour out his comments and reflections, and fill, with an extraordinary solicitude, page after page with elucidations, explanations, justifications, of the vanished incidents of a remote past. He would snip with scissors the pages of ancient journals, and with delicate ecclesiastical fingers, drop unknown mysteries into the flames.

Sometimes he would turn to the four red folio scrapbooks with their collection of newspaper cuttings, concerning himself, over a period of thirty years. Then the pale cheeks would flush and the close-drawn lips would grow even more menacing than before. 'Stupid, mulish malice,' he would note. 'Pure lying—conscious, deliberate and designed.' 'Suggestive lying. Personal animosity is at the bottom of this.'

And then he would suddenly begin to doubt. After all, where was he? What had he accomplished? Had any of it been worthwhile? Had he not been out of the world all his life! Out of the world!

'Croker's "Life and Letters", and Hayward's "Letters",' he notes, 'are so full of politics, literature, action, events, collision of mind with mind, and that with such a multitude of men in every state of life, that when I look back, it seems as if I had been simply useless.'

And again, 'The complete isolation and exclusion from the official life of England in which I have lived, makes me feel as if I had done nothing'. He struggled to console himself with the reflexion that all this was only 'the natural order'. 'If the natural order is moved by the supernatural order, then I may not have done nothing. Fifty years of witness for God and His Truth, I hope, has not been in vain.' But the same thoughts recurred. 'In reading Macaulay's life I had a haunting feeling that his had been a life of public utility and mine a vita umbratilis, a life in the shade.' Ah! it was God's will. 'Mine has been a life of fifty years out of the world as Gladstone's has been in it. The work of his life in this world is manifest. I hope mine may be in the next. I suppose our Lord called me out of the world because He saw that I should lose my soul in it.' Clearly, that was the explanation.

And yet he remained sufficiently in the world to discharge with absolute efficiency the complex government of his diocese almost up to the last moment of his existence. Though his bodily strength gradually ebbed, the vigour of his mind was undismayed. At last, supported by cushions, he continued, by means of a dictated correspondence, to exert his accustomed rule. Only occasionally would he lay aside his work to plunge into the yet more necessary duties of devotion. Never again would he preach; never again would he put into practice those three salutary rules of his in choosing a subject for a sermon: '(1) asking God to guide the choice; (2) applying the matter to myself; (3) making the sign of the cross on my head and heart and lips in honour of the Sacred Mouth;' but he could still pray; he could turn especially to the Holy Ghost.

'A very simple but devout person,' he wrote in one of his latest memoranda, 'asked me why in my first volume of sermons I said so little about the Holy Ghost. I was not aware of it; but I found it to be true. I at once resolved that I would make a reparation every day of my life to the Holy Ghost. This I have never failed to do to this day. To this I owe the light and faith which brought me into the truefold. I bought all the books I could about the Holy Ghost. I worked out the truths about His personality, His presence, and His office. This made me understand the last paragraph in the Apostles' Creed, and made me a Catholic Christian.'

So, though Death came slowly, struggling step by step with that bold and tenacious spirit, when he did come at last the Cardinal was ready. Robed in his archiepiscopal vestments, his rochet, his girdle, and his mozzetta, with the scarlet biretta on his head, and the pectoral cross upon his breast, he made his solemn Profession of Faith in the Holy Roman Church. A crowd of lesser dignitaries, each in the garments of his office, attended the ceremonial. The Bishop of Salford held up the Pontificale and the Bishop of Amycla bore the wax taper. The provost of Westminster, on his knees, read aloud the Profession of Faith, surrounded by the Canons of the Diocese. Towards those who gathered about him, the dying man was still able to show some signs of recognition, and even, perhaps, of affection; yet it seemed that his chief preoccupation, up to the very end, was with his obedience to the rules prescribed by the Divine Authority. 'I am glad to have been able to do everything in due order', were among his last words. 'Si fort qu'on soit,' says one of the profoundest of the observers of the human heart, 'on peut eprouver le besoin de s'incliner devant quelqu'un ou quelque chose. S'incliner devant Dieu, c'est toujours le moins humiliant.'

Manning died on January 14th, 1892, in the eighty-fifth year of his age. A few days later Mr. Gladstone took occasion, in a letter to a friend, to refer to his relations with the late Cardinal. Manning's conversion was, he said,

'altogether the severest blow that ever befell me. In a late letter the Cardinal termed it a quarrel, but in my reply I told him it was not a quarrel, but a death; and that was the truth. Since then there have been vicissitudes. But I am quite certain that to the last his personal feelings never changed; and I believe also that he kept a promise made in 1851, to remember me before God at the most solemn moments; a promise which I greatly valued. The whole subject is to me at once of extreme interest and of considerable restraint.'

'His reluctance to die,' concluded Mr. Gladstone, 'may be explained by an intense anxiety to complete unfulfilled service.'

The funeral was the occasion of a popular demonstration such as has rarely been witnessed in the streets of London. The route of the procession was lined by vast crowds of working people, whose imaginations, in some instinctive manner, had been touched. Many who had hardly seen him declared that in Cardinal Manning they had lost their best friend. Was it the magnetic vigour of the dead man's spirit that moved them? Or was it his valiant disregard of common custom and those conventional reserves and poor punctilios which are wont to hem about the great? Or was it something untameable in his

glances and in his gestures? Or was it, perhaps, the mysterious glamour
lingering about him, of the antique organisation of Rome? For whatever cause,
the mind of the people had been impressed; and yet, after all, the impression
was more acute than lasting. The Cardinal's memory is a dim thing today. And
he who descends into the crypt of that Cathedral which Manning never lived
to see, will observe, in the quiet niche with the sepulchral monument, that the
dust lies thick on the strange, the incongruous, the almost impossible object
which, with its elaborations of dependent tassels, hangs down from the dim
vault like some forlorn and forgotten trophy—the Hat.